MASONRY

Homeowner **SURVIVAL GUIDE**

MASONRY

The DIY Guide to Working with Concrete, Brick, Block, and Stone

skills institute press

Distributed By
Fox Chapel Publishing

FOX CHAPEL
PUBLISHING

© 2012 by Skills Institute Press LLC
"Homeowner Survival Guide" series trademark of Skills Institute Press.
Published and distributed in North America by Fox Chapel Publishing Company, Inc., East Petersburg, PA.

Masonry is an original work, first published in 2012.

Portions of text and art previously published by and reproduced under license with Direct Holdings Americas Inc.
ISBN 978-1-56523-698-1

Library of Congress Cataloging-in-Publication Data

Masonry. -- First.
     p. cm. -- (Homeowner survival series)
Includes index.
ISBN 978-1-56523-698-1 (pbk.)
1. Masonry--Amateurs' manuals.
TH5313.M3522 2012
693'.1--dc23

                              2011041873

To learn more about the other great books from Fox Chapel Publishing, or to find a retailer near you, call toll-free 800-457-
                    9112 or visit us at www.FoxChapelPublishing.com.

Note to Authors: We are always looking for talented authors to write new books. Please send a brief letter
             describing your idea to Acquisition Editor, 1970 Broad Street, East Petersburg, PA 17520.

                         Printed in China
                          First printing

Table of Contents

What You
Can Learn

Masonry Techniques,
page 8
Whether building a brick barbecue or a stone archway, the first step for the new mason is learning to work with new mortar and stone and to repair the old material that they have.

Concrete, page 50
Pouring concrete for a sidewalk or driveway takes a certain precision but can easily be learned.

Mastering Rugged Materials, page 112

Choosing the right bricks or stones is an important first skill to learn in building a structure to be proud of.

Building with Brick, Block, Tile, and Stone, page 146

Beyond standard masonry skills, you will need a few simple techniques to finish these projects.

CHAPTER 1

Masonry Techniques

The projects in this book involve techniques that take only a bit of practice to master. Most of them can be learned while you are making repairs to existing brickwork or concrete. In this chapter, we'll show you how to make simple repairs to walls and paving, as well as how to work with masonry.

Stone and brick can be used to build walls, stairs, and patios that will last with little maintenance, but a savvy homeowner will know how to make the minor repairs necessary to enjoy these features for years.

A Masonry Tool Kit

Working with brick, stone, concrete, and tile requires a number of specialized tools. Pictured below and opposite are the most common ones; others are shown throughout the book. The majority of these tools is available at hardware stores, and some large power tools—a vibratory tamper, for instance—can be rented.

For most masonry projects, you'll also need standard layout and measuring tools such as a 50-foot-long tape measure. A mason's level or long carpenter's level is essential for checking for level and plumb. For laying out corners, you'll need a carpenter's square.

Pointing trowel
This small trowel is ideal for replacing damaged mortar in a brick wall or shaping mortar joints.

Quarry-tile trowel
The flat edge is used to spread a bed of mortar for setting tile on a concrete slab. The toothed edge is used to comb the bed; the size of the teeth determines the depth of the bed.

Joint filler
The long, thin blade is handy for packing mortar into joints in walls and paving.

Mason's trowel
This large trowel is the basic tool for laying a mortar bed for a brick or block wall as well as for spreading mortar on the units.

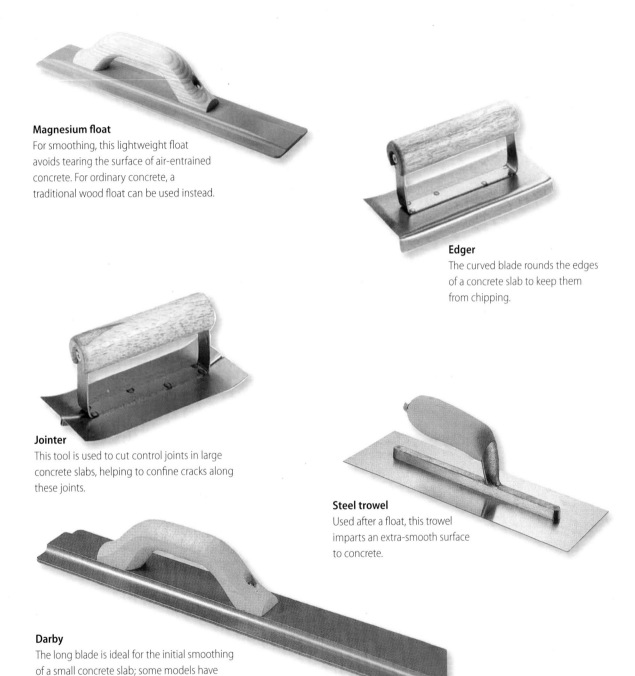

Magnesium float
For smoothing, this lightweight float avoids tearing the surface of air-entrained concrete. For ordinary concrete, a traditional wood float can be used instead.

Edger
The curved blade rounds the edges of a concrete slab to keep them from chipping.

Jointer
This tool is used to cut control joints in large concrete slabs, helping to confine cracks along these joints.

Steel trowel
Used after a float, this trowel imparts an extra-smooth surface to concrete.

Darby
The long blade is ideal for the initial smoothing of a small concrete slab; some models have two handles.

Brick set
Strike this tool with a ball-peen hammer to score and cut bricks and stone.

Stone chisel
Strike this chisel with a ball-peen hammer to score and cut flagstone.

Joint chisel
This tool is struck with a ball-peen hammer to chip damaged mortar from the joints between bricks. A cold chisel can be used instead.

Hawk
During small repairs to brick, this tool is handy for holding mortar close to the job.

Ball-peen hammer
This hammer is for striking metal tools such as brick sets and joint chisels where a standard hammer might be damaged.

Mortar hoe
This is the traditional tool for mixing mortar and concrete by hand. A shovel can be used instead.

Stonemason's hammer
The pointed end of this heavy hammer is ideal for trimming small pieces of stone.

Mason's line blocks
The wood blocks grip the corners of a wall, while the cord forms a guideline for laying brick courses.

Working with Mortar

Mortar is the material that bonds bricks, stones, and blocks together. Once you master mixing and troweling mortar, you can fix walls or paving, or launch more ambitious projects such as building a brick wall or laying a walk.

PREPARING THE MIX

Mortar consists of Portland cement, sand, hydrated lime, and water. Cement and lime are packaged dry in bags, and the sand should be a clean, fine type called masonry sand—never use beach sand. You can substitute masonry cement (a premeasured mix of cement and lime) for the total amount of cement and lime. Or, buy prepackaged mortar mix; while it is more expensive than buying the separate ingredients, it is more convenient for small jobs. You can also buy colored Portland cement to make mortar that accents joints between bricks or disguises repairs.

Recipes for making 1 cubic foot of dry mortar mix are listed opposite. Type N is suited for most purposes; Type M is best for below-grade work and paving; and Type S is recommended for regions with seismic activity. Mortar can be prepared by hand *(next page)*, but you can rent a power mixer for large jobs. Start by preparing 1 cubic foot at a time. You can increase this amount as you learn how much you can comfortably use before the mix hardens.

SPREADING TECHNIQUES

A mason's trowel is used to lay a bed of mortar for bricks, blocks, or stones, and to spread mortar on these units. While working, stir the mortar often. If it dries out, add water from time to time to restore its workability; but discard mortar that starts to set before it is spread.

FINISHING JOINTS

After the mortar has set but before it hardens—usually under an hour or when it will just hold a thumbprint—you can finish the joints *(pages 22–23)*. Only the joint styles that shed water well are recommended for most outdoor use. Nonwaterproof joints should be reserved for indoor projects or dry climates.

TOOLS
- Wheelbarrow
- Mortar hoe
- Mortar board
- Mason's trowel
- Mason's level
- Convex jointer
- V-shaped jointer
- Raking tool
- Pointing trowel

MATERIALS
- Mortar ingredients (Portland cement, masonry sand, hydrated lime)
- Bricks or concrete blocks

SAFETY TIP

Mortar—both wet and dry—is caustic. Wear gloves and long sleeves when applying it and add goggles and a dust mask when mixing mortar. Put on hard-toed shoes when handling bricks.

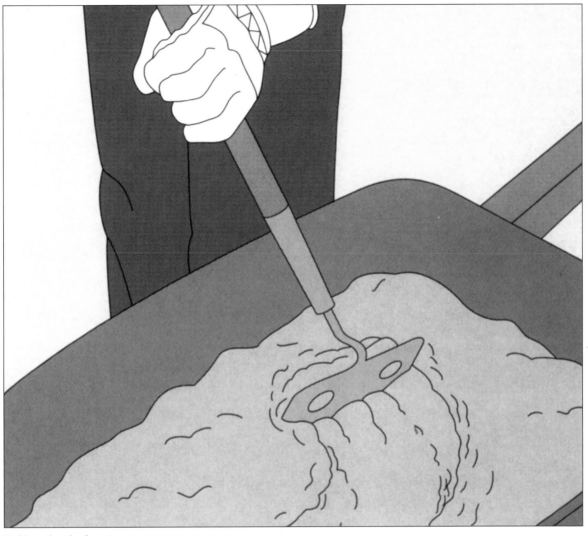

Making a batch of mortar

At least 4 to 5 gallons of water are generally required for 1 cubic foot of mortar. Be prepared to make adjustments as you test the consistency of the mix. Measure the dry ingredients into a wheelbarrow, and mix thoroughly with a mortar hoe. Push the mixture to one end of the wheelbarrow and pour 2½ to 3 gallons of water into the other end. Hoe the dry ingredients into the water. Working back and forth, gradually add more water and mix until the mortar has the consistency of soft mush and there are no lumps. Test the mix by plowing a curved furrow across the surface with the hoe (above). If the sides of the furrow stay in place and the clinging mortar can be shaken off the hoe freely, the mix is ready. If the sides of the furrow collapse, the mix is too wet—add a small amount of the dry materials and retest. If the mortar does not shake freely off the hoe, it is too dry—add very small amounts of water.

MAKING A MORTAR BED

Loading the trowel

With a mason's trowel, scoop mortar from the wheelbarrow and form a mound in the center of a mortar board or a square piece of plywood. Grasping the trowel handle between thumb and forefinger, drop the edge of the trowel to separate a slice of mortar from the mound *(right, top)*. With a twist of the wrist, sweep the trowel blade under the slice and scoop up a wedge of mortar onto one side of the blade *(right, bottom)*. Keeping the blade flat, shake the trowel vigorously to flatten the mortar.

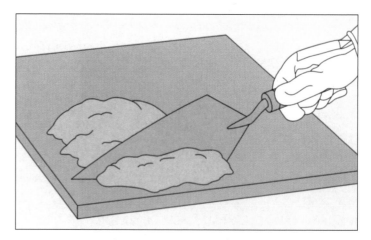

Mortar Recipes

Type	Portland Cement	Hydrated Lime	Sand
M	2½ gal.	½ gal.	7½ gal.
N	1¼ gal.	1¼ gal.	7½ gal.
S	2½ gal.	1¼ gal.	8¾ gal.

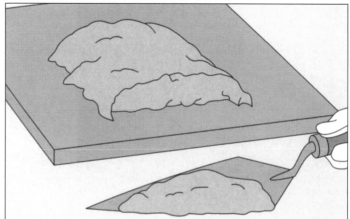

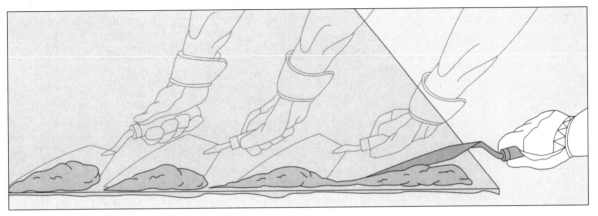

Throwing a line of mortar

You'll need one line—or bed—of mortar to lay a row of bricks; throw two lines for concrete blocks. Set the point of the trowel at the point where you want to begin the mortar bed. Pull the trowel toward you and at the same time rotate the blade counterclockwise 180 degrees *(above)*; the mortar will roll off and form a straight line—about one brick wide, a few bricks long, and 1 inch thick. If the line is not straight, return the mortar to the board and try again. Practice until you are able to form a mortar bed three bricks long with one smooth motion.

Furrowing the mortar

Immediately after throwing the mortar bed, cut a shallow depression down the center with the point of the trowel *(right)*. By spreading the mortar out slightly from the center, the furrow allows the mortar to be evenly distributed when the brick is pressed down on it.

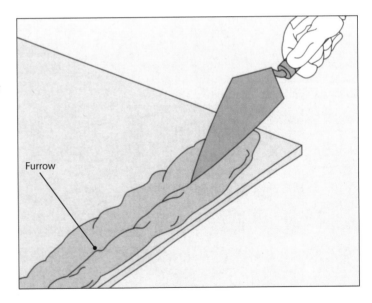

Furrow

LAYING BRICKS

Beginning a row

Starting just inside one end of the mortar bed, push the brick down about ½ inch into the mortar. With a mason's level—or a long carpenter's level—check that the brick is level—both across its width and length *(right)*—and plumb. If it's not, tap it with the trowel handle and check again. You may need to remove the brick and reset it in the bed to get it in the correct position.

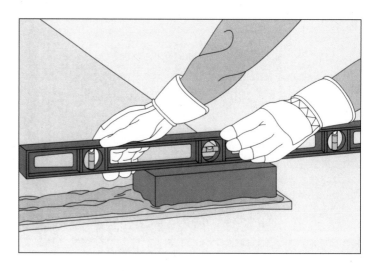

Buttering successive bricks

For all bricks between the ends of a row, spread—or butter—¾ inch of mortar on any surface that will adjoin previously laid bricks. Scoop up enough mortar to cover the surface and spread it on. For end-to-end bricks, cover an end *(left)*; for side-to-side bricks, cover one side. Remove any mortar that slides onto an adjoining surface.

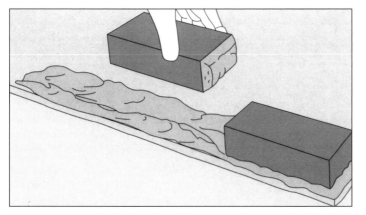

Continuing the row

Set the brick in the mortar bed with the buttered end aligned with the end of the first brick *(left, top)*. With one motion, push the brick down ½ inch into the bed and against the first brick so there is ½ inch of mortar between them. With the edge of the trowel, trim off mortar that squeezed out of the joints *(left, bottom)* and return it to the mortar board. Continue laying bricks until you reach the middle of the row, as determined by the dry run when planning the layout *(page 159)*, then work from the opposite end until there is room for a final brick in the middle.

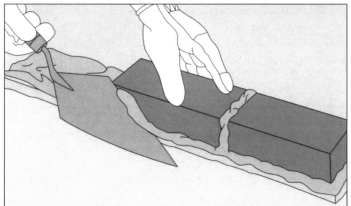

Laying the closure brick

Butter the exposed ends of the bricks on each side of the middle of the row and both ends of the last brick—called the closure brick. Gently lower the closure brick into the opening *(right)*. Push the brick into the mortar bed and trim off excess mortar.

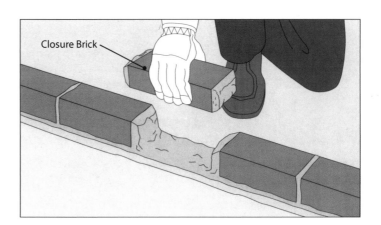

Closure Brick

FINISHING JOINTS

Concave joint

This popular joint keeps moisture out and, since mortar is forced tightly between the bricks, makes an excellent bond. Shape it by pressing the mortar firmly with anything curved that fits between the bricks—a convex jointer *(photograph)*, a dowel, a metal rod, or even a spoon.

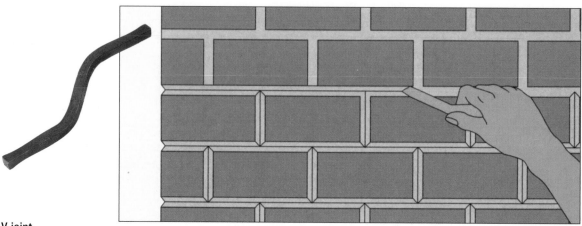

V-joint

Form the sharp, water-shedding line of this mortar joint with a V-shaped jointer *(photograph)*, a piece of wood, or the tip of a pointing trowel.

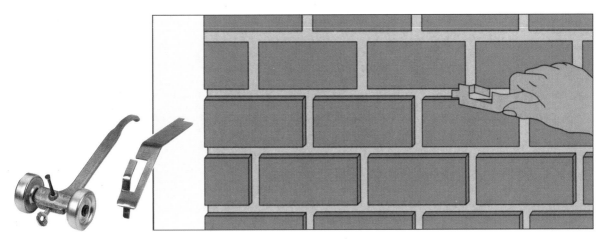

Raked joint

With its deep recess, this joint is not water-resistant, but it casts a dramatic shadow that accentuates the rows of bricks. Shape the joint by removing ¼ inch of mortar and smoothing the surface with a raking tool—a wheeled type can also be used *(photograph)*.

Weathered joint

This is a water-shedding joint that is recessed from bottom to top. Hold the blade of a pointing trowel at an angle and compress the mortar starting from the front edge of the brick below the joint upward to a point ¼ inch inside the brick above.

Struck joint

Although this joint is not water-resistant because its recess slants from top to bottom, it produces dramatic shadows. To shape it, hold the blade of a pointing trowel at an angle and compress the mortar from the front edge of the top brick to a point ¼ inch inside the front of the bottom brick.

Flush joint

The easiest of all joints to form, this type is neither strong nor water-shedding because the mortar is not compacted. It is made by simply troweling off excess mortar flush with the surface of the bricks.

Extruded joint

Also called a weeping joint, an extruded joint gives a rustic appearance to a wall. However, it is a poor choice for areas exposed to strong winds, heavy rain, or freezing temperatures because the mortar is not compacted. Create extruded joints by applying excess mortar; when the bricks are laid, some mortar squeezes out and hangs down. You can reproduce the effect when repointing by adding mortar along the joints (right).

Repairs to Brick

For a masonry structure to survive—especially in cold regions—cracks and crumbled sections must be repaired promptly. Water that infiltrates the brick and mortar can cause damage as it freezes and thaws. The techniques shown here for repairing brick apply to paths and patios as well as walls—only the orientation of the work is different.

MORTAR JOINTS AND BRICKS

Crumbling mortar joints are repaired by a process called pointing—chiseling out the old mortar and packing in new (pages 26–27). For damaged bricks, replace the bricks and mortar (pages 28–29); finish the joints to match existing ones (pages 22–24). To piece in a new brick, you may need to cut it to fit (page 28).

CRACKS IN WALLS

Closely inspect any crack in a brick wall—it can be a sign of foundation movement. A crack is usually not serious if its edges are no more than ⅛ inch apart, parallel, and aligned. Such cracks can be filled using the pointing technique; you may want to color the mortar to match the brick. If a crack is wider than ⅛ inch, or its edges are misaligned (not matched in shape or position), serious structural problems may exist—consult a building professional.

TOOLS	MATERIALS
■ Joint chisel	■ Mortar ingredients: Portland cement, masonry sand, hydrated lime
■ Ball-peen hammer	
■ Hawk	
■ Pointing trowel	■ Replacement bricks
■ Joint filler	
■ Ruler	
■ Brick set	

SAFETY TIP

Dry or wet, mortar is caustic, so protect your hands with gloves, and put on a dust mask when mixing mortar. Always wear goggles when mixing or chipping out mortar and when splitting bricks. Wear gloves when splitting or handling rough bricks.

RENEWING DETERIORATING MORTAR

Cleaning out the joint

With a joint chisel (or a cold chisel) and a ball-peen hammer, chip out crumbling mortar from the joints to a depth of at least 1 inch *(above)*. Brush or blow the joints clean.

Packing in new mortar
Dampen the joints with a wet brush or a garden hose set to a fine spray. Spread a ½ inch-thick mound of mortar onto a hawk. For a short joint, slice off a thin wedge of mortar with the bottom edge of a pointing trowel and press it into the joint *(above, left)*.

For long horizontal joints, use a joint filler; align the hawk flush with the opening and push in the mortar *(above, right)*. When the mortar is firm enough to hold a thumbprint, finish the joints to match the wall *(pages 22–24)*.

SPLITTING A BRICK

Scoring and cutting

With a pencil and ruler, mark a cutting line across both side edges of the brick; mark on the diagonal if this shape is required. Set the blade of a brick set—beveled edge facing the waste portion of the brick—on the cutting line. Tap the handle with a ball-peen hammer to score the line *(right)*. Repeat to score the cutting line on the opposite edge. Lay the brick on a bed of sand with the waste part of the brick pointing away from you. Insert the brickset into the scored line, again with the bevel facing the waste, and strike the handle sharply to split the brick.

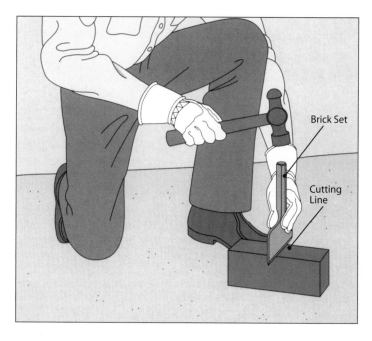

Brick Set

Cutting Line

REPLACING A BROKEN BRICK

Fitting in a new brick

Chisel out the mortar surrounding the damaged brick *(page 26)*. Chip out the brick with a brick set and ball-peen hammer, then brush the space clean. Select a brick that fits the slot or cut one to fit *(above)*. Dampen the slot's surfaces and apply a ¾-inch coating of mortar with a pointing trowel. Hold the brick on a hawk about ½ inch above the row and push the brick into the slot. Trowel in extra mortar if needed to fill the joints *(page 27)*. When the mortar is firm enough to hold a thumbprint, finish the joints to match the wall *(pages 22–24)*.

FILLING IN A DAMAGED WALL

Cutting out and replacing bricks

Remove the mortar surrounding the damaged bricks *(page 26)* and chip out the bricks with a brick set and a ball-peen hammer *(above, left)*. It may be necessary to remove bricks above the damage as well. Brush away debris. Dampen all surfaces of the replacement bricks and their openings in the wall. Lay mortar beds for the bricks, troweling and furrowing the bed as you would for new bricks *(page 20)*. Butter the bricks and lay them in place on the mortar beds *(above, right)*. When the mortar is firm enough to hold a thumbprint, finish the joints to match the wall *(pages 22–24)*.

Mending Concrete

Paradoxically, concrete surfaces cannot be repaired with concrete—the coarse gravel aggregate in the new concrete would prevent a strong bond between the patch and the surrounding area. Instead, it's best to use mortar or commercial epoxy or latex patching compounds designed for concrete repairs.

SURFACE PREPARATION

Remove damaged concrete and all dirt, debris, and standing water, and keep the area damp for several hours—preferably overnight.

FILLING CRACKS

For cracks up to ⅛ inch wide, use a latex or epoxy patching compound. Force it into the crack with a putty knife or a mason's trowel, and smooth it level with the surrounding concrete.

Mend larger cracks with mortar prepared without lime *(pages 31–33)*. You can also use a latex or epoxy patching compound and apply it in a similar way.

SPALLING

Surfaces on which the concrete has flaked off in thin scales—a condition called spalling—are best patched with an epoxy patching compound *(page 33)*.

REPAIRING STEPS

Large broken pieces of steps can be glued back into place with an epoxy patching compound *(page 34)*. But when sections of the stairs crumble away, you will have to build them up again with mortar *(pages 36–38)*.

CURING

A mortar patch must cure slowly and in the presence of moisture. Let the patch set for about two hours, then cover it with a sheet of plastic. On a horizontal surface, the cover can be secured by bricks or rocks; for vertical surfaces, use tape. Over the next three days, lift the cover daily and sprinkle water on the patch. If a vertical patch cannot be covered conveniently, moisten it twice a day. For latex and epoxy compounds, check the product label for curing instructions.

TOOLS
- Cold chisel
- Ball-peen hammer
- Paintbrush
- Mason's trowel
- Steel trowel
- Sledgehammer
- Wire brush
- Putty knife
- Circular saw
- Stair edger

MATERIALS
- Mortar ingredients: Portland cement, masonry sand
- Epoxy concrete-patching compound
- Scrap lumber bricks

SAFETY TIP
Wear gloves when repairing concrete, and goggles when breaking up a damaged surface.

FILLING WIDE CRACKS

Removing damaged concrete
With a cold chisel and a ball-peen hammer, chip
away all cracked or crumbling concrete to about
1 inch below the surface *(above)*.

Undercutting the edges

To provide a better bond and keep the patch from heaving upward after the job is done, undercut the edges of the crack: Chisel at an angle to make the hole wider at the bottom than at the top *(inset)*. Remove all rubble and dirt. Soak the crack with water for several hours; if possible, run a trickle from a garden hose over it overnight.

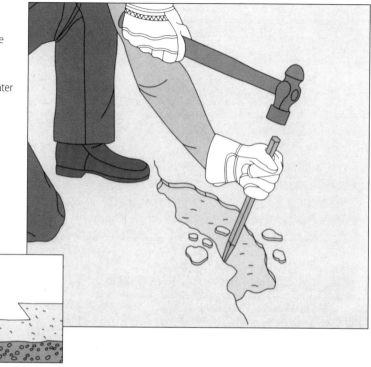

Preparing the crack

Prepare the mortar by mixing 1 part Portland cement and 3 parts masonry sand, adding enough water to make a paste stiff enough to work with a mason's trowel. Make a small batch of cement paint by adding water to Portland cement until it has the consistency of thick paint. Coat the edges of the crack with the cement paint *(left)*; then, proceed immediately to complete the repair before the paint dries.

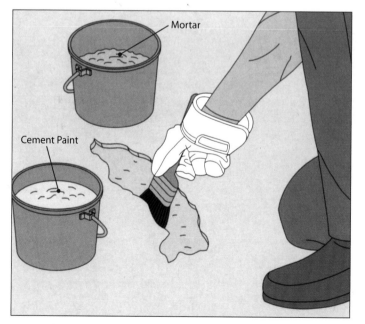

Mortar

Cement Paint

Mending the crack

Pack the mortar firmly into the crack with a mason's trowel, cutting deep into the mixture to remove air pockets. Level the mortar with a steel trowel. Let the patch stand for an hour, then spread it evenly across the surface, sliding the trowel back and forth with its leading edge raised *(left)*.

TREATING SPALLED SURFACES

Using an epoxy mix

Break up large areas of scaling concrete with an 8-pound sledgehammer *(right)*—don't slam the tool against the surface; let its own weight provide the force. A rotary hammer with a bush hammer head *(page 34)* is an alternate tool for the job; for small areas, a ball-peen hammer and a cold chisel will be adequate. Sweep up dust and debris; dislodge small fragments with a stiff wire brush. Soak the damaged area with water and keep it wet for several hours, preferably overnight. The area should still be damp when you apply the patch. Prepare a commercial epoxy patching compound for concrete and apply it with a steel trowel. Bring the new layer level with the surrounding concrete, and feather it thinly at the edges. Let the patch stand for 24 hours before letting it support any weight.

A POWER TOOL TO BREAK UP CONCRETE

A rotary hammer—available at tool rental shops—produces a rapid chiseling action similar to a jackhammer; a side handle provides a sturdy grip. Rotary hammers come with a variety of heads—for a concrete slab, choose a bush hammer head, as shown. Since the tool is relatively small, you may prefer a jackhammer equipped with a bush hammer head for a large job.

A rotary hammer is also handy for boring holes in masonry—replace the bush hammer head with a masonry core bit, similar to a hole saw—and a flip of a switch provides the drilling action.

GLUING A BROKEN STEP

Gluing the chip
Brush particles of dirt and cement from the broken piece and the corner of the step. Mix a small batch of epoxy patching compound for concrete; then, with a mason's trowel, spread some onto the chipped part of the broken piece. Hold the piece firmly in place until the compound hardens; you can prop a board against the piece to hold it in place *(right)*.

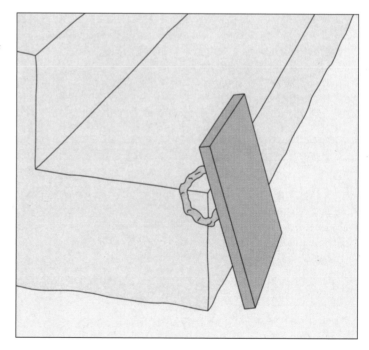

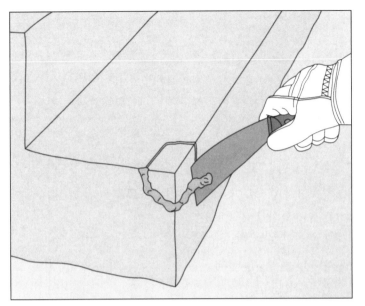

Completing the job

Once the compound has set, use a putty knife to scrape away any excess that has oozed out between the piece and the step *(left)*. If a small crack remains around the repair, pack patching compound into the crack with a trowel, then smooth the patch level. Avoid touching the repaired corner for at least 24 hours.

REBUILDING A CORNER

Shaping a replacement piece

Clean the corner and keep it damp for several hours, preferably overnight. Mix 1 part Portland cement with 3 parts masonry sand and add just enough water to make a mortar paste that holds its shape. With a mason's trowel, apply the mortar to the damage, roughly shaping it. Let the patch harden until it is firm enough to hold a thumbprint.

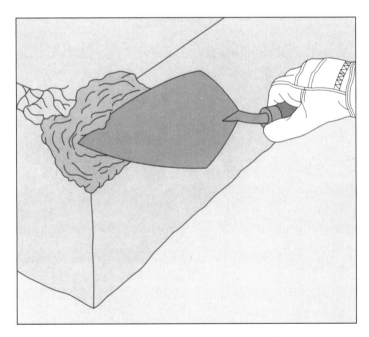

Finishing the corner
Finish and smooth the corner flush with the steps with a steel trowel *(right)*. Let the mortar cure for at least three days, and avoid putting weight on the corner for a few days afterward.

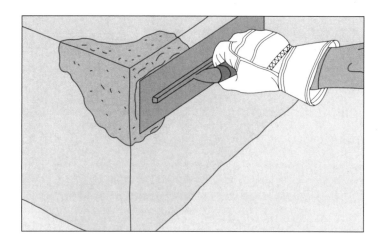

REPAIRING A CHIPPED EDGE

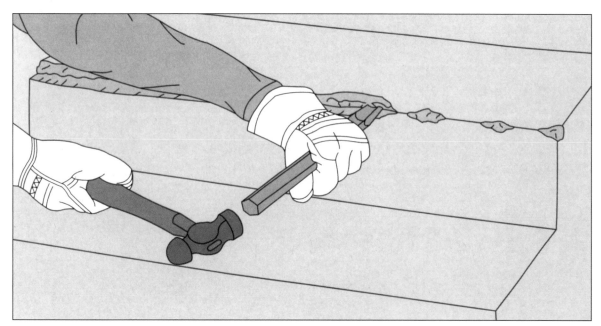

Clearing the damage
With a cold chisel and a ball-peen hammer held horizontally, chip off the damaged concrete all the way across the edge of the step.

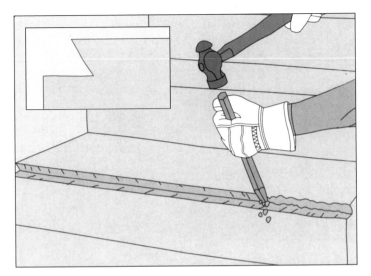

Undercutting the groove

Holding the chisel at an angle, chip away enough of the edge to make a V-shaped groove *(inset)*. Clean away the debris and keep the edge damp for several hours, preferably overnight.

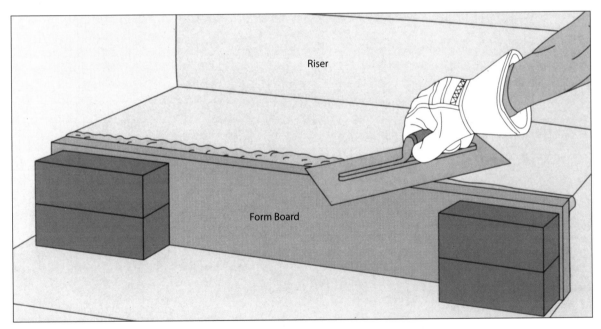

Riser

Form Board

Rebuilding the edge

Cut a board to the length and height of the riser and set it against the step as a form board. Hold it in place with bricks or concrete blocks. Mix 1 part Portland cement with 3 parts masonry sand, then add just enough water to make a mortar paste that holds its shape. Coat the groove with cement paint *(page 32)*, then immediately fill it in with the mortar, using a steel trowel to shape it and smooth it flush with the step and form board *(above)*.

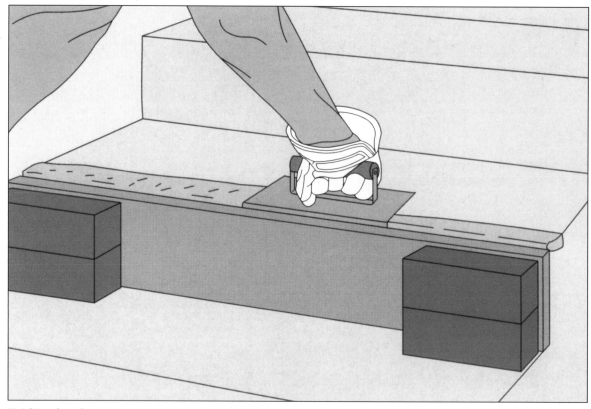

Finishing the Job

Once the mortar is thumbprint hard, round the edge of the step with an edger *(above)*, then carefully remove the form board. Let the mortar cure for at least three days, then avoid stepping on the edge for a few more days.

First Aid for Holes in Asphalt

The asphalt used to cover driveways and walks is a mixture of gravel with a crude-oil extract as a binder. This material can develop cracks and holes from frost, water, and traffic; it also absorbs oil and other automotive drippings.

PATCHING HOLES

A type of filler called cold-mix asphalt is manufactured in two varieties: cut-back and emulsified. Either product works well in dry holes, but damp holes require the emulsified type. Both types are sold in airtight bags or buckets, usually containing enough material to patch about 1½ square feet of surface.

When the temperature is below 40° F, do not patch or seal asphalt. If cool weather has hardened the cold-mix into an unworkable lump, soften it by placing the container in a heated area for a few hours before use.

SEALING THE SURFACE

To protect asphalt from deterioration and from absorbing oil and automobile fluids, coat it once every four or five years with a waterproof and petroleum-resistant sealer containing sand for skid resistance. Simply pour the product onto the surface and spread it evenly with a push broom or squeegee.

The sealer will fill cracks up to ⅛ inch wide. For cracks up to ½ inch wide, clean out soil and debris, then pour ready-to-use crack filler into the cavities. If a crack is up to 1 inch wide, thicken the filler with sand to a puttylike consistency, then push the mixture into the crack with a putty knife.

TOOLS
- Shovel
- Circular saw and masonry blade

MATERIALS
- Cold-mix asphalt
- Sand
- 4 x 4
- Door handles
- Wood screws

SAFETY TIP

Wear gloves when working with cold-mix asphalt.

USING COLD MIXES

Preparing the hole

With a shovel, dig out the hole to a depth of 3 or 4 inches and remove any loose material. Cut back the edges of the hole with a circular saw and a masonry blade until you reach sound asphalt, making the sides of the hole vertical. Compact the bottom of the hole with a tamper made by screwing a pair of large door handles to opposite sides of a 4-by-4 (above).

Patching the hole

Pour cold-mix asphalt into the hole, filling it halfway. Slice through the asphalt with a shovel to release air pockets (above), then compact it with the tamper. Complete the patch by adding 2-inch layers of coldmix, tamping each one, until it is even with the surrounding surface. On a driveway, build up the patch ½ inch higher than the surface, since the weight of a car will flatten it. Spread sand over the patch until it dries (usually about two days) to keep it from sticking to footwear.

Homemade Concrete in Convenient Batches

Concrete's great strength comes from its materials: gravel (called coarse aggregate), sand, and cement. The coarse aggregate supplies bulk, the sand fills voids between the aggregate, and the cement, when moistened with water, binds the sand and aggregate into a durable solid.

AIR-ENTRAINED CONCRETE

For most projects, you can use ordinary concrete. But in an area subject to freezing, large projects, such as building a concrete patio or steps, require air-entrained concrete, which contains additives that produce and trap microscopic air bubbles. When the concrete dries, the bubbles form tiny spaces within the slab so it can expand and contract with a minimum of cracking.

MIXING CONCRETE

It's best to buy sacks of premixed dry ingredients to which you simply add water. One 60-pound bag will make about ½ cubic foot of concrete. The amount of water required for a concrete recipe is critical; even a small amount of extra water can weaken the concrete. The approximate amount of water will be indicated on the bag, but add it only a little at a time, and be sure to test the consistency as described on page 43.

A small amount of plain concrete (about 2½ cubic feet) can be mixed by hand in a wheelbarrow *(page 42)* or on any flat surface. Unlike ordinary concrete, the air-entrained type must be machine mixed; buy a small quantity of the additive from a concrete supplier and rent a gasoline- or electric-powered mixer. The mixer will enable you to pour and finish about 16 square feet of a slab 4 inches thick before the concrete becomes too hard to finish. If you need more, arrange for a truck to deliver ready-mix concrete *(page 59)*.

TOOLS	MATERIALS
■ Mortar hoe	■ Premixed concrete
■ Square shovel	
■ Bucket	
■ Wheelbarrow	

SAFETY TIP

Wet or dry, concrete is caustic—wear gloves, goggles, and a dust mask when mixing concrete.

AN EXTRA INGREDIENT: COLOR

Concrete, though normally gray, can be colored by several methods. You can paint or stain the concrete after it cures, but it will have to be repainted as the color wears away. You can also apply a dust-on pigment while the concrete is still wet. The color is applied in two coats and the surface is floated before and after each application. This pigment is inexpensive but can be tricky to apply evenly. An alternative to these methods is to add pigment to the concrete mixture. Although more expensive than the other techniques, the color is distributed evenly and is permanent. If you order ready-mix concrete, you can request that it be precolored.

Adding color to concrete requires machine mixing; simply add synthetic pigments or natural metallic oxides to the dry concrete in the power mixer. Synthetic pigments cost more, but are less likely to bleach or fade; both types come in a range of colors you can use directly or combine to produce custom shades. To keep coloring uniform from batch to batch, measure all ingredients by weight, not volume; and never add more than 10 percent pigment—it will weaken the concrete. A bathroom scale wrapped in plastic is ideal for weighing. Concrete lightens as it dries, so you may need to experiment to find the right amount of pigment.

PREPARING CONCRETE

Premixd Concrete

Mixing in a wheelbarrow

Empty the premixed dry ingredients into a wheelbarrow. With a mortar hoe, push the mixture to the sides to form a bowl-like depression. Slowly pour about three quarters of the required quantity of water into the depression. Pull the dry materials from the edges of the ring into the water, working all around the pile until the water is absorbed by the mixture. When no water remains standing on the surface, turn the concrete over with the hoe three or four times. Add water a little at a time until the mixture completely coats all the coarse aggregate. Leave any unused water in the bucket until you test the consistency of the concrete, then make any necessary corrections (page 43).

TESTING THE CONSISTENCY

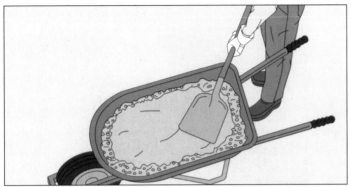

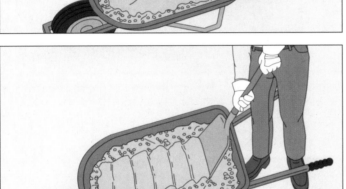

Judging and correcting the mix

Smooth the concrete in the wheelbarrow by sliding the bottom of a square shovel across the concrete's surface *(top)*. Jab the edge of the shovel into the concrete to form grooves. If the surface is smooth and the grooves are distinct, the concrete is ready to use *(bottom)*. If the surface roughens or the grooves are indistinct, add a small amount of water. If the surface is wet or the grooves collapse, add a small amount of dry ingredients. Retest the batch until the consistency is correct.

CLEANING UP AFTER THE WORK IN DONE

Most sanitation departments will not haul away leftover concrete or mortar. Generally, you have to take it yourself to the nearest dump. For easier handling, pour it into paper bags, or pile it in small heaps on sheets of paper and let it set into manageable lumps. You can also mold concrete and save it for future use—for example, keep simple 2-by-4 wood forms ready for pouring excess concrete while it is still workable, and cast stepping-stones.

Clean tools at the end of each work session. Put all tools in a wheelbarrow and hose them down. Do not dump dirty water into your drainage system or into a city street or sewer. Instead, dig a large hole, pour the dirty water in, and fill the hole.

Hose out a power concrete mixer at day's end. (Many rental companies charge an extra fee for a mixer that comes back dirty.) If you cannot clean the drum completely with a hose, turn the mixer on and pour in a mixture of water and two shovelfuls of gravel to scour it out. Empty the mixer after three or four minutes, then hose it out again. If you have waited too long to clean the mixer, you may have to scrape bits of hardened concrete out with a wire brush or chip them off with a chisel.

MIXING BY MACHINE

If you're mixing more than 3 cubic feet of concrete, it's worth renting an electric or gas-powered mixer. A typical electric mixer holds 6 cubic feet, but they are available in capacities up to 12 cubic feet.

Set up the mixer near your work site and make sure it is level and wedged in place.

To make concrete from premixed dry ingredients, empty the dry ingredients and about half the water into the mixer. Turn on the mixer for about three minutes. Then add air-entrainment additive, if needed, and gradually add more water until the mixture completely coats the coarse aggregate and the concrete is a uniform color.

Test a few shovelfuls in a wheelbarrow *(page 43)*, and return the test batch to the mixer before making corrections. When the concrete is thoroughly mixed, clump the contents into a wheelbarrow and hose out the drum. When you finish using the mixer, clean up as described on page 43.

CAUTION

Never reach into the mixer or insert tools while it is turning. Never operate an electric mixer in damp conditions, and cover it when not in use. Fuel a gas-powered mixer only when the engine is off and has cooled down.

Removing Stains and Blemishes

Ordinary scrubbing with detergent and a stiff fiber brush gets most blemishes off brick and concrete; if this method fails, they may need special treatments with chemicals available from a pharmacy, home-improvement or garden center, or a pool-supply store. Moss can usually be removed from brick and concrete with ammonium sulfamate. Wash slate, granite, or bluestone with a gentle laundry detergent. For limestone and sandstone, avoid detergents; instead, use clean water and a scrub brush.

Efflorescence

Smoke

Efflorescence and smoke
The white, powdery deposit known as efflorescence can be cleaned from brick with a commercial product formulated for brick. On concrete or block, as a last resort, apply a 1-to-10 solution of muriatic acid, but don't leave it on the surface more than a few minutes. For colored concrete, dilute the solution to 1-to-100. Scrub off smoke residue with a scouring powder containing bleach, then rinse with water.

Oil

Paint

Brown Stain

Rust

Oil, tar, and stains

Apply a commercial emulsifying agent to oil or tar on brick, then hose it off with water. For stubborn tar, add kerosene to the agent. On concrete or block, apply a degreaser, available at auto-supply stores. Let it stand for the time recommended, then wipe it off. For brown stains caused by the manganese used for coloring brick, wet the brick and brush it with a solution of 1 part vinegar, 1 part hydrogen peroxide, and 6 parts water. For green stains caused by the vanadium salts in the brick, use a solution of 1 pound of potassium or sodium hydroxide and 1 gallon of water; leave it on for two or three days, then rinse it off. Or use a commercial product formulated for either type of stain.

Paint and rust

To remove paint, apply a commercial water-based paint remover; clean it off with a scraper or a wire brush, then wash the surface with water. To get rust off brick, spray or brush the brick with a strong (1 pound per gallon of water) solution of oxalic acid, then hose it off. On concrete or block, scrub it with a stiff brush and a solution of 1 part sodium citrate, 7 parts glycerin, and 6 parts lukewarm water; then rinse it thoroughly.

Fastening to Masonry

Many home improvement projects, such as putting up a porch railing, installing outdoor wiring, or running a water pipe to an outside faucet, involve anchoring to masonry. The fastener you choose depends partly on the object you are mounting and partly on the type of masonry. Screws and expansion anchors, toggle bolts, steel masonry nails, and a family of glues called mastics are the principal types of fasteners.

MASONRY NAILS

For relatively light loads such as furring strips for paneling, use masonry nails. The nails can be driven by hand or by a powder-actuated hammer *(page 49)*, which uses gunpowder to fire the nails. Some are activated by a trigger; others must be struck with a hammer. Follow the manufacturer's directions exactly when using this tool. Brick and stone are too hard for nailing into except at mortal joints.

MASTICS

These glues, which are simply spread on the masonry surface, give added strength to masonry nails. They can be used on concrete or block, but brick and stone make poor surfaces for gluing.

EXPANSION ANCHORS AND TOGGLES

Expansion anchors—consisting of a screw and an anchor—are suitable for concrete and the solid parts of blocks. They can be fastened into mortar joints and in brick, if you are careful not to tighten the screw so much that the material around the edge of the hole begins to crumble. In stone, expansion anchors are unsatisfactory: They can create stresses that will cause cracks. For this material—and any solid masonry where a very strong fastener is required—a technique employing bolts is useful *(page 48)*. Toggles—consisting of a bolt and threaded wings—are suited best for the hollow parts of concrete blocks.

MAKING THE HOLES

Toggles and anchors fit into predrilled holes. Small holes can be made in concrete block with a carbide-tipped masonry bit in an electric drill. Holes larger than 1 inch need a four-edged chisel called a star drill. For small holes in harder materials such as concrete, brick, or stone, consider renting an electric hammer drill *(page 48)*. Holes larger than 1 inch in hard materials need a rotary hammer with a masonry core bit *(page 49)*.

TOOLS	MATERIALS
■ Carpenter's level	■ Masking tape
■ Utility knife	■ Bolts, washers, nuts
■ Putty knife	■ Epoxy
■ Rubber mallet	■ Power fasteners
■ Powder-actuated hammer	
■ Electric drill	

SAFETY TIP

Always wear goggles when drilling or nailing into masonry; add earplugs when using a powder-actuated hammer.

A HAMMER AND DRILL ALL IN ONE

To make small holes in solid masonry—brick, stone, or concrete—you may want to rent a hammer drill *(right)*, fitted with a carbide-tipped bit. This tool can pound a bit into masonry about 3,000 times per minute. A depth rod indicates when the hole is deep enough.

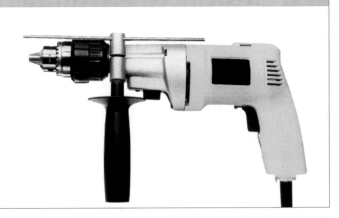

ANCHORING STUDS WITH BOLTS

Setting a bolt in epoxy

Mark and drill holes for the bolts, then dust off the masonry near the holes. Insert a bolt headfirst into each hole and, with a putty knife, fill the space around the bolt with epoxy. Cut a strip of 2-inch-wide masking tape for each bolt and, with a utility knife, slice Xs in the center of the strips. Stick the tape firmly to the wall, with the bolt projecting through the X *(left)*; the tape keeps the bolt centered in the hole and the epoxy from oozing out. Allow the epoxy to cure for the length of time specified by the manufacturer.

Fastening a stud to the bolts

Holding one side of the board you are mounting against the bolts, plumb the board with a carpenter's level. Over each bolt, strike the board sharply with a rubber mallet *(left)*, indenting the wood slightly. Drill a hole through the board at each mark. Fasten the board to the bolts with washers and nuts.

A POWDER-ACTUATED HAMMER

Loading and firing

Push the fastener into the muzzle *(right, top)*. Insert the power load into the chamber. Hold the tool at 90 degrees to the surface and push the muzzle against the surface, compressing the spring. Strike the firing pin straight on with a sharp blow from a 1-pound hammer *(right, bottom)*.

CAUTION

This tool contains explosives—keep it out of the reach of children.

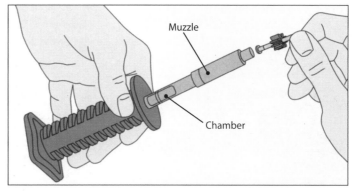

Muzzle

Chamber

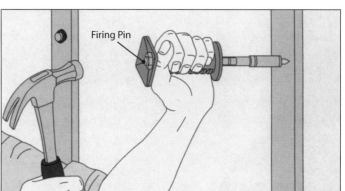

Firing Pin

CHAPTER 2

Concrete

Concrete is the most versatile masonry material—it can be molded into any shape within the forms you build. The basic slab-casting techniques found in this chapter can be applied to create a number of projects ranging from a patio to a set of stairs. And the final result need not be drab—a simple slab can be broken up into a grid, colored, or textured in a number of different ways.

Consider the myriad possibilities before laying a simple concrete patio, whether it be accented with tile, formed curves, or bricks.

What Goes Wrong and Why

When a concrete slab is well poured and finished, it is nearly indestructible; but incorrect preparation, pouring, or finishing can result in the surface defects shown in these photographs. While most problems can be detected at a glance, dusting is most readily identified by touching the surface with your finger to see if the deteriorated cement is easily picked up.

A common cause of surface defects is an incorrect concrete mixture. Too much water or too much cement will weaken the entire slab. If you use aggregate containing soft stones or clay lumps instead of hard gravel, the surface may break down under normal wear and weather.

Excessive floating or darbying is a primary cause of surface failure. Such overworking sends aggregate toward the bottom of the slab and brings too much water and cement toward the top. When the top of the slab contains too little aggregate, which provides strength, the surface may break up.

Another cause of surface damage is improper curing—letting a slab dry out or freeze and thaw too soon after the concrete has been poured.

Cracking
Large cracks like those at right open up in concrete that contains too much water, or that was poured too rapidly to be compacted properly. You can avoid cracking by forcing freshly poured concrete into all corners of the form with a shovel. Do not let a batch of concrete dry before pouring the next batch against it—cracks may appear at the junction. Proper compaction of the base prior to the pour and control joints added to the fresh concrete also help prevent cracking. Cracks in concrete can be repaired as described on page 30.

Scaling
A concrete mixture containing too much water will lack strength once it has cured, causing the top layer to crumble or scale *(left)*. Scaling also occurs where concrete with no air-entrainment additive is used in a freezing climate, or where a slab is subjected to freezing and thawing or deicing compounds before it has cured properly. Deicing products containing ammonium sulfate or ammonium nitrate can sometimes cause scaling even when a slab has cured properly.

Crazing

A network of hairline cracks may appear on the surface of a concrete slab that contains too much cement *(right)*; such mixtures shrink excessively as they dry. Improper curing will also cause crazing.

Popouts

If the aggregate contains lumps of clay or crumbly stones, these soft elements will deteriorate and wash away when the concrete has dried, leaving surface holes called popouts *(left)*. Popouts can be filled with latex or epoxy concrete-patching compounds, or mortar.

Spalling

If the surface of a slab is weakened by too much darbying or troweling, thin layers of concrete will flake away—a condition called spalling *(right)*. You can patch a spalled surface with an epoxy concrete-patching compound, as illustrated on page 33.

Dusting

Improper curing or overworking a slab with a darby or float can weaken the top layer of a slab to such an extent that you will be able to pick up powdered cement from the surface on your finger *(left)*. To halt this deterioration, brush the surface thoroughly to remove loose material, then apply a concrete sealer—an acrylic-polymer compound available at most paint stores. One gallon will cover about 400 square feet.

Preparing for the Project

Before starting a job, check your local building codes. Codes and zoning laws may dictate the project's dimensions, location, and design, as well as the quality standards the materials must meet. In some cases, you may need a building permit. Adhering to these rules can often help you avoid costly mistakes.

INSPECTING THE SITE

When you are designing a walk, wall, or patio, take into account the slope of the ground; any rock outcroppings, ponds, or streams; the trees, shrubs, and their roots; and the location of gas, electric, water, or sewage lines and of dry wells, septic tanks, or cesspools—including abandoned ones. Then draw a scaled layout that shows existing structures and landscape features.

TESTING THE SOIL

For a concrete slab, dig a test hole about 1 foot deep and inspect the soil. Unless the earth is very sandy and well drained, the slab will need a 4-inch gravel or sand drainage bed under it to keep the concrete dry and permit it to shift without cracking when the earth freezes and thaws.

Footings for walls must extend below the frost line. Dig a hole to this depth to check the soil. For both slabs and footings, the ground must be stable. Avoid any site with more than 3 feet of recent landfill. If you strike water in the test hole, or if you live in an earthquake zone, consult a professional.

PREPARING THE GROUND

Before excavating, clear the area by moving plants and, if necessary, getting rid of old concrete. To break up concrete that is not reinforced with wire mesh, lift and drop a heavy sledgehammer onto it, working from the edges toward the center. For a large area, consider renting a jackhammer; call in a professional for reinforced concrete. With the site cleared, consult your preliminary drawings and lay out the design with a string or garden hose.

ORDERING MATERIALS

For a small project, or one you plan to divide into sections with permanent forms, you can make your own concrete *(pages 41–43)*. For projects requiring more than about 2 cubic yards of concrete, you may want to order ready-mix concrete *(page 59)*.

Ready-mix concrete, gravel, and sand are sold by the cubic yard. Estimate the length, width, and depth of the project and calculate its volume, keeping in mind that there are 27 cubic feet in a cubic yard. Or, simply divide the cubic feet by 25—resulting in cubic yardage with an allowance of about 8 percent for waste. The chart on page 58 provides the number of cubic yards of materials required for both 4-and 6-inch-thick slabs or drainage beds.

Estimating Materials for Concrete Slabs

Area of slab	Thickness of slab	
	4 in.	6 in.
10 sq. ft.	.12 cu. yd.	.18 cu. yd.
25 sq. ft.	.32 cu. yd.	.48 cu. yd.
50 sq. ft.	.64 cu. yd.	.96 cu. yd.
100 sq. ft.	1.28 cu. yd.	1.92 cu. yd.
200 sq. ft.	2.56 cu. yd.	3.84 cu. yd.
300 sq. ft.	3.84 cu. yd.	5.76 cu. yd.
400 sq. ft.	5.12 cu. yd.	7.68 cu. yd.
500 sq. ft.	6.4 cu. yd.	9.6 cu. yd.

Calculating cubic yards

For most residential applications, a 4-inch slab is adequate; a slab that is thinner than this may crack. If you are building a driveway that will be used by delivery trucks, make the slab 6 inches thick. Once you have determined the desired area of the slab, use the table at left to determine the number of cubic yards of concrete, gravel, or sand required for a slab or drainage bed either 4 or 6 inches thick. Add about 8 percent for waste and spillage.

ORDERING READY-MIX CONCRETE

For large jobs, it is easiest to buy the concrete from a ready-mix company that will make it to your specifications and deliver it ready to be poured. But when the truck arrives, you will have to work fast and probably enlist several assistants.

When ordering the concrete, tell the dealer how many cubic yards you need (above) and describe how you want to use it. In industry jargon, most jobs will call for 5½- to 6-bag concrete—made with about 520 to 560 pounds of cement for each cubic yard. Where winters are severe, use 6-bag concrete; elsewhere 5½-bag is adequate.

Professionals measure the consistency of wet concrete by the number of inches a cone-shaped mass will slump when a conical form is lifted off. You will need concrete with a 4- to 6-inch slump. Concrete with less than 4 inches of slump is too stiff to be workable; with more than 6 inches, it becomes soupy and the concrete will fail. Also, ask for a coarse aggregate (gravel) with a maximum size of 1 inch diameter and for a 6 percent air entrainment in freezing climates; 4 percent elsewhere.

How much you pay depends on the size of your order. If you need more than 3 to 4 cubic yards of concrete, you may find that ready-mix costs less than mixing the concrete yourself. If you need less than this, you may have to pay a delivery charge or a higher price per cubic yard. Most prices include 30 to 45 minutes' delivery time. If the truck stays longer while you unload it, you will generally pay an hourly rate for the extra time.

To speed up delivery, decide in advance where the truck will stop and how you will get the concrete to the work site. Having the truck drive up onto your property is seldom advisable. The weight of the truck can break a curb, driveway, or sidewalk and make deep ruts in your lawn. If the time and work saved are worth the risk, however, you can minimize the damage by laying 2-inch-thick planks along the truck's route to equalize the load. However, never let the truck drive over a septic tank or cesspool.

Usually, the best plan is to have the truck park on the street and use chutes and wheelbarrows to unload the concrete. A 10- to 12-foot chute is standard equipment on most trucks. Some companies also provide large hoses to pump concrete from the truck directly to the building site. This is an expensive option, but handy for hard-to-reach sites.

Unloading ready-mix

Organize a crew of helpers ahead of time. Have some of them place the fresh concrete, and others smooth and finish the slab. Set a 4-by-8 plywood panel where the truck will discharge the concrete. Then place 2- foot-wide plywood strips or 1-by-8 planks from the unloading area to your work site to make a track for the wheelbarrows—the type with a pneumatic tire—and prevent the wheels from sinking into the lawn. When the truck arrives, work quickly with a shovel to slide the concrete from the delivery chute into each wheelbarrow (above), taking care not to overfill it. Do not leave concrete in the chute—it may drop out before you return. As you work, shift the wood track to the most convenient point for dumping the wheelbarrow loads.

CAUTION

A chute or wheelbarrow full of concrete is extremely heavy. Agree on signals with the truck operator and your helpers before the pour begins, and keep children away from the truck.

Forms for Slabs

Forms serve as molds for concrete, holding it to shape as it cures. Generally, forms are assembled on site before the concrete is poured and removed after it has cured; but some can remain in the slab as permanent decorative features *(page 87)*.

STAKING AND GRADING

The first step is to lay out the slab with stakes. These are cut 18 inches long from 1-by-2s or 2-by-2s. The stakes support the forms and indicate the grade, or pitch, of the slab, which ensures it will shed water. For a walkway that will run in a straight line over ground that slopes gently away from the house, follow the natural slope. If the ground doesn't slope at all, grade the slab from side to side to ensure proper drainage. A lot that slopes abruptly requires a slab with steps.

EXCAVATING

With the stakes in place, the site is excavated, leveled, and compacted. The required depth of the excavation depends on local codes; but for structures like walkways, patios, steps, and driveways, 8 inches is generally sufficient to accommodate the thickness of the slab and 4 inches of gravel beneath it.

BUILDING FORMS

A straight form for a simple 4-inch-thick slab, such as a walkway *(page 62)* or patio, is made from 1-by-4s or 2-by-4s. For curved sections, flashing metal can be used *(page 69)*.

The best choices for temporary form boards are fir, pine, or spruce. Buy wood that is planed smooth on all its surfaces and, unlike lumber used in most construction, green (unseasoned). Fully dried wood may absorb moisture from the concrete and interfere with curing. Permanent forms can be made of redwood, cedar, or pressure-treated wood. Use single boards for each side of the form, if possible, but long sections can be pieced together by butting boards end to end and reinforcing the seams with stakes.

GRAVEL AND EXPANSION JOINTS

After the forms are assembled, a gravel drainage bed is laid in place and leveled *(page 70)*. Before the concrete is poured, expansion-joint material is added against any adjoining structure, such as steps, a wall, or another slab, so the new slab can shift independently *(page 70)*.

TOOLS		MATERIALS
■ Ruler	■ Handsaw	■ 1 x 4s, 1 x 8
■ Maul	■ Circular saw	■ 2 x 4s
■ Shovel	■ Tin snips	■ Stakes
■ Flat spade		■ String
■ Rake		■ Sand
■ Tamper		■ Gravel
■ Line level		■ Common nails (½", 3")
■ Mason's level		■ Flashing metal
■ Hammer		■ Expansion-joint material

SAFETY TIP

Protect your eyes with goggles when hammering or driving in stakes.

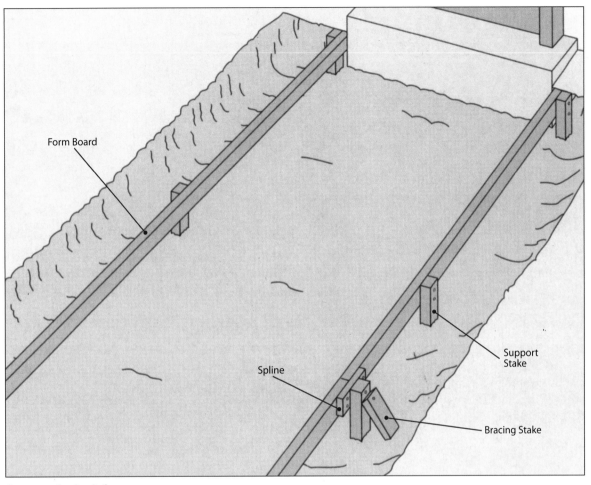

Form Board

Support Stake

Spline

Bracing Stake

Anatomy of a simple form

After the walk is outlined and the site excavated, support stakes are set at both ends—¾ inch or 1½ inches outside the proposed slab to allow space for 1-by-4 or 2-by-4 form boards—and at 3- to 4-foot intervals in between. Form boards are nailed to the stakes, leaving room for a 4-inch gravel bed under the slab. The stakes are sawed off even with the top of the form boards. The joints between form boards are reinforced with splines and with diagonally set bracing stakes.

EXCAVATING THE BASE

Sand

Outlining the slab

For a straight slab, drive stakes at each corner of the proposed slab with a maul.
Tie a string to each stake at one end of the proposed slab and run it to the stake
at the opposite end. Mark the string lines on the ground by trickling an unbroken
line of sand along each one *(above)*. For a curved slab, use the technique on
page 69 to position stakes around the curve.

Digging the trench
Remove the stakes and strings. Dig a trench of the required depth to about 1 foot outside the sand lines *(above)*. If you plan to reuse the turf later along the edge of the finished slab, cut it out with a flat spade and save it.

Leveling the base

Smooth the base of the trench with a rake. Remove any large rocks and fill in the holes with sand or gravel. Flatten the base by pulling a 2-by-4 as long as the base is wide across the surface *(right)*.

Tamping the base

Compact the soil with a cast iron tamper *(left)*. For a large project, rent a vibratory tamper *(page 83)*. Fill low spots with gravel and tamp again. With the 2-by-4, check that the bottom of the trench is even across its width; add gravel and tamp again as necessary.

STAKING THE SITE

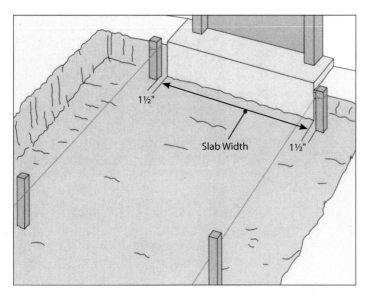

1½"

Slab Width   1½"

Driving support stakes

Drive the corner stakes again—this time about 6 inches deep—positioning them outside the desired slab by the thickness of the form boards (1-by-4s or 2-by-4s). Mark the end stakes at each end of the slab at ground level. Tie strings between the end stakes, running the strings along the insides of the stakes. Drive support stakes at 3- to 4-foot intervals between the end stakes along both sides of the slab so their insides lie against the strings, as shown at left. If there is a curve in the walkway, do not set the stakes for the curve until the form boards for the straight sections have been added.

GRADING A WALKWAY ON A SLOPING LOT

Marking the lengthwise grade

The form boards on a gently sloping site can follow the slope of the land. However, you'll need to compensate for minor rises and dips: Mark the intermediary stakes level with the string lines *(above)*. Repeat for the stakes along the other side of the walkway.

SLOPING A WALKWAY ON A FLAT SITE

Leveling one set of stakes

Hang a line level at the middle of the string and raise the low end of the string until the string is level, and at ground level. Mark the intermediary stakes level with the string.

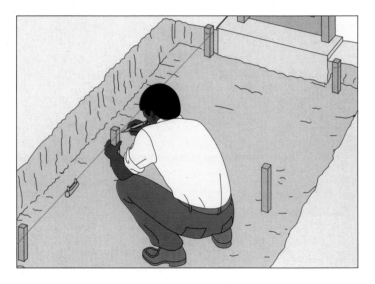

Grading the slab across its width

Nail one end of a long straight board the width of the slab to the marked end stake, level with the mark. Use a single nail so the board can pivot. Place a level on the board to level it and mark the opposite stake *(above)*. Remove the board and mark a second line below the one you just marked so the slab will slope from side to side ¼ inch for each foot of width. Repeat for the pair of stakes at the opposite end of the walkway. Run a string between the two end stakes you've just marked and mark the intermediary stakes level with the string.

ATTACHING FORM BOARDS

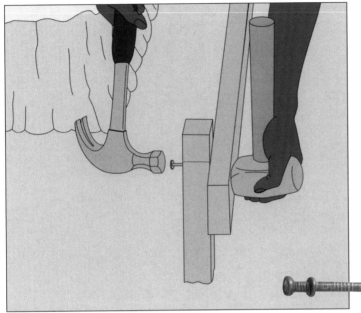

Nailing the boards to the stakes

Starting on one side of the excavation, hold an end of a form board against the inside edge of the stake nearest the house—flush with the top of the stake on sloping ground; flush with the grading line on flat ground. With a 3-inch common nail—not galvanized, so it can be pulled easily—fasten the board to the stake, cushioning the blows with a maul *(left)*. Alternatively, you can use double-headed nails *(photograph)*, which are easily removed. Nail the board to the stake at its opposite end, then to the stake at its middle. Drive a second set of nails below the first. Attach the board to any intermediate stakes. Where form boards meet end to end, nail a spline across the joint on the outside faces of the boards, then drive an additional support stake behind the spline.

Making corners

At a corner, butt the form board against the back face of the one already in place. Fasten the board to the support stake, holding its top edge level with the first board *(right)*.

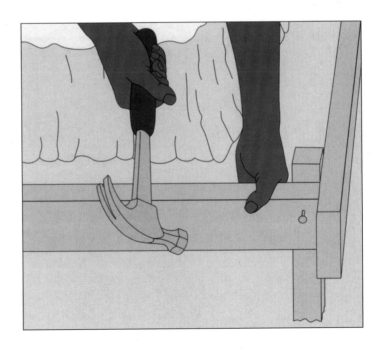

Adding braces

At each corner and end joint between form boards, drive a bracing stake into the ground on an angle so it presses against the back of the support stake below the nails. Nail the braces to the support stakes (right).

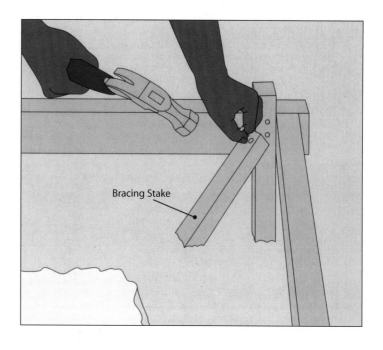

Bracing Stake

Trimming the stakes

Cut off the part of the support stakes that extends above form boards to provide a uniformly flat surface for screeding the slab later.

SHAPING CURVES WITH METAL

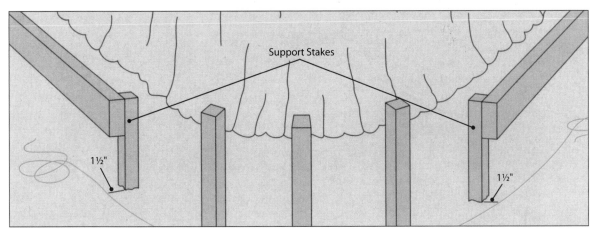

Support Stakes

1½"

1½"

Staking curves

Lay string or a garden hose in the desired arc 1½ inches inside the support stakes at the start and end of the curve. Drive support stakes for the curve about every foot along the string or hose, as shown above. Tie a string between the stakes at each end of the curve so it is level with the grading marks on the stakes. Pull the string taut and mark a grading line on each stake along the curve where the string crosses it, then remove the string.

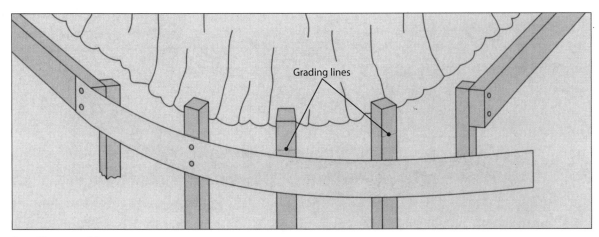

Grading lines

Attaching curved forms

With tin snips, cut a strip of flashing metal 4 inches wide and 6 inches longer than the curve. Overlapping the form boards at the ends of the curve by 3 inches, line up the top of the strip of metal with the boards and the grading marks on the support stakes. Attach the strip to the stakes with ½-inch common nails. Add a bracing stake behind each support stake *(page 68)*, then trim the tops of the support stakes level with the form boards and strip of metal. Backfill the trench outside the curve for extra support, taking care not to tamp the earth so hard that you move the stakes.

LAYING A DRAINAGE BED

Placing gravel

Shovel a 4-inch layer of gravel into the forms. Make a bladed screed from a 2-by-4 long enough to extend over the form boards and a 1-by-8 or 2-by-8 as long as the space between the form boards. Fasten the boards together as shown above so that the 4-inch "blade" fits down between the form boards. Level the gravel bed from one end to the other by pulling the screed, blade-down, toward you and running the ends on the form boards *(right)*—the blade will reach down ½ inch lower than the bottom of the form boards. Fill in any low spots with gravel. Compact the bed with a tamper, adding more gravel if necessary. Then level the surface again with the screed.

Screed

DEALING WITH JOINTS

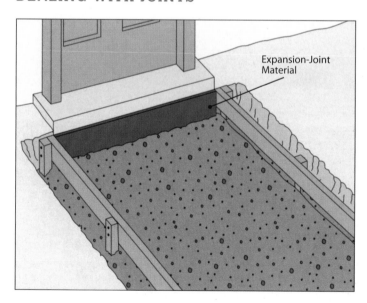

Expansion-Joint Material

Installing joint filler

For each structure adjoining the new slab, cut a piece of expansion-joint material—usually asphalt-impregnated fiberboard—to a width of 4 inches and long enough to fit snugly between the form boards. Place a piece against each structure flush with the top of the form boards, as shown at left.

Pouring and Finishing the Slab

On the day of the pour, have everything ready to go and in place before the ready-mix truck arrives. A fresh mix needs to be poured and finished in about three hours; after that, it becomes too stiff to be workable. In that time, one person, working alone with ready-mix concrete, can place and finish about 30 feet of a 3-foot-wide walkway. One helper will make it possible to lay 50 feet of walk in the same time; two helpers, 70 feet.

POURING THE CONCRETE

Moisten the forms, and in hot weather, the gravel base as well. Once the concrete is placed, compact, level, and then smooth it. Working the concrete, as described below, forces "bleed" water to the surface; do not work the mixture further until the water disappears. For air-entrained concrete on a hot dry day, the water will likely evaporate completely in 10 to 20 minutes; in cool or humid weather, an hour or more may be needed.

FINISHING

Once the bleed water disappears, the surface can be finished and the edges rounded to reduce the chance of chipping *(page 74)*. Incise control joints in the slab *(page 75)* at intervals of 24 times the thickness of the slab (every 8 feet for a 4-inch slab) to induce cracks at the joints rather than at random. These joints are not needed in footings. If you want the marks of the edger and jointing tool to be visible, finish the surface with the desired texture first. Otherwise, do the edges and joints before finishing.

Next, finish the slab with a float and trowel *(pages 75–76)*. For a nonslip surface, required for an exterior slab, you can either stop after floating—resulting in a less finished appearance—or trowel the slab and then roughen the surface with a broom *(page 76)*. Other decorative finishes—embedded stones and imitation flagstone—are shown on page 77.

CURING

Keep concrete damp and undisturbed for at least a week after finishing to allow the chemical reactions that give it strength to proceed *(page 79)*. After curing, the forms can be removed, but keep heavy loads off the surface for an additional week. If you plan to paint or stain the concrete, allow it to cure for 6 weeks first.

TOOLS		MATERIALS
■ Square shovel	■ 2 x 8 guide board	■ Polyethylene sheeting
■ Flat spade	■ Carpenter's square	■ Bricks
■ 2 x 4 screed		■ Burlap sacks
■ Darby	■ Magnesium or wood float	
■ Pointing trowel	■ Steel trowel	
■ Edger	■ Stiff-bristle broom	
■ Jointer		

SAFETY TIP

Wet concrete is caustic—don gloves when working with it. If you are mixing concrete, put on goggles and a dust mask. Wear goggles when pouring or screeding concrete to protect your eyes from splashes. Goggles and rubber gloves protect you from splashes when washing a slab with muriatic acid.

PLACING THE CONCRETE

Filling the forms

Dump the first wheelbarrow load of concrete into the forms—those farthest from the truck if you are using ready-mix. With square shovels, pack the concrete into the corners of the forms, being careful not to knock down or completely submerge the expansion-joint material. Shovel each successive load up against the preceding one, overfilling the forms by about ½ inch. Thrust the shovel edge through the concrete as you work it to eliminate air pockets.

Clearing the edges
As soon as one section of forms is completely filled, drive a flat spade down between the concrete and the inside surface of the forms to force large pieces of aggregate away from the edges of the slab *(left)*.

Compacting and leveling
Use the edge of a straight 2-by-4 or 2-by-6, about 2 feet wider than the forms, as a screed. Zigzag the screed from side to side across the slab *(right)*. If you plan to embed stones in the surface of the slab, follow the instructions on page 77 after screeding.

Smoothing the surface

Working quickly, smooth the concrete and eliminate any "hills" or depressions with a darby. Pressing down lightly on the trailing edge of the darby, sweep it back and forth across the surface in wide arcs to force large aggregate down into the concrete *(right)*. When bleed water floats to the surface, stop darbying. Wait until the water evaporates and the shiny surface dulls, then immediately begin edging and jointing the slab and finishing the surface *(right)*. If you plan to create a flagstone finish, do so now, following the instructions on page 78.

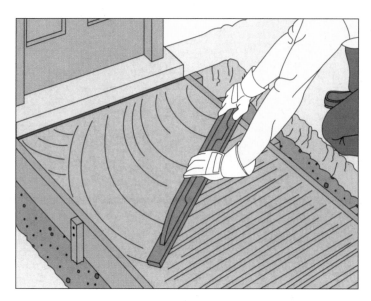

FINISHING TOUCHES

Rounding the edges

Draw a pointing trowel along the inside edges of the forms to cut the top inch or so of concrete away from the wood *(above, left)*. Finish the sides of the slab by running an edger with a ½-inch radius firmly back and forth along the edges until they are smooth and rounded *(above, right)*.

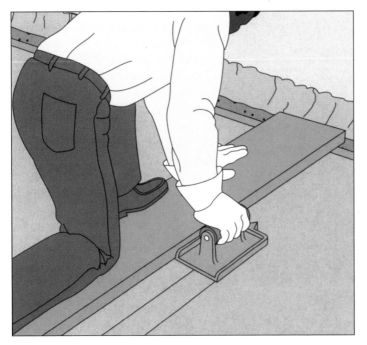

Cutting control joints

At each point where you wish to produce a joint, set a 2-by-8 as a guide board across the forms; check with a carpenter's square to ensure the board is perpendicular to the edges of the slab. With a jointer that has a radius of ¼ to ½ inch and will cut to a depth of one quarter the slab's thickness—1 inch in this case—press down into the concrete along the edge of the guide board. Run the tool back and forth to cut the joint *(left)*.

Floating the surface

For concrete with an air-entrainment additive, smooth and compact the concrete with a magnesium float; otherwise, use a wood float. Starting at one end of the slab, press the float flat on the surface and sweep the blade back and forth in gentle curves *(right)*. Support yourself on a second float to lean over the concrete, or use knee-boards *(page 87)*. Move backward as you work toward the slab's opposite end to remove any hand or knee prints in the concrete. Do not overwork the concrete; this will drive aggregate down and bring water and cement to the surface, weakening the slab.

Troweling the surface

To further smooth and compact the surface, use a steel trowel. Keep the blade nearly flat and sweep the trowel back and forth in arcs 2 to 3 feet wide *(right)*.

Creating a nonslip surface

Beginning at one end of the slab, draw a stiff-bristle broom straight across the surface *(left)*; for a curved pattern, move the broom in arcs. If the broom picks up small lumps of concrete, hose the broom clean and let the slab dry a few minutes longer before proceeding. If you have to press down heavily to score the surface, work quickly, before the concrete becomes too hard.

DECORATIVE FINISHES

A broomed surface *(page 76)* is only one way to finish a concrete patio or walkway. Shown on this page are two attractive alternatives: embedded multicolored stones and simulated flagstone; the stones help to make the surface more slip-resistant. You can also pattern a concrete surface with commercial stamps that make impressions in the concrete, imitating the outlines of brick, stone, or tile.

Embedding stones

This finish is easy to achieve by adding stones to a freshly poured concrete slab. Buy round multicolored stones, ¾ to 1¼ inch in diameter, called aggregate, or ⅜-inch pea gravel, from a masonry supplier.

After compacting and leveling the concrete *(page 73)*, wet the stones and drop them onto the surface at random or in a pattern. Tap the stones down with a darby until the tops are just below the surface *(right)*; if they sink too far, wait for the concrete to firm up. Then, after the bleed water disappears, place a board over the slab. When you can stand on the board without pushing the stones farther down, brush the concrete with a stiff-bristled broom to expose just the top third of each stone. Flush away excess concrete with a fine spray from a hose.

Begin curing the concrete *(page 79)*; after a day or two, uncover the slab and wash the stones with 1 part commercial-strength muriatic acid added to 10 parts water. Continue curing it for another five or six days.

CAUTION

Pour acid into water—never pour water into acid.

DECORATIVE FINISHES

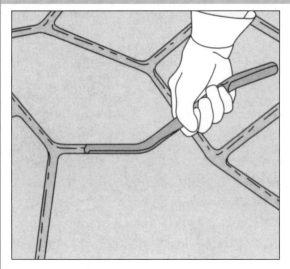

Imitating flagstones

After smoothing the concrete with a darby *(page 74)*, carve irregularly spaced grooves ½ to ¾ inch deep into the surface with a convex jointer *(above)*. Alternatively, use a bent length of copper pipe. When the bleed water evaporates, float the concrete *(page 75)* and reshape the grooves until the flagstonelike pattern shows distinctly. Then, brush out any remaining bits of concrete from the grooves with a dry paintbrush.

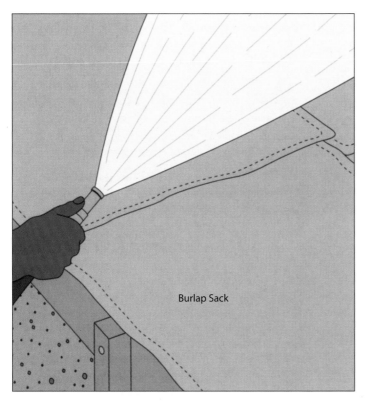

Burlap Sack

Keeping the concrete damp

To ensure proper curing of the concrete, keep it damp for a week. For footings, this can be accomplished by covering the surface with polyethylene sheeting weighted down with bricks; however, this method may stain the surface. For a walk or patio, cover the concrete with clean, soaking-wet burlap sacks and keep the burlap damp by spraying it periodically with a hose *(left)*. Alternatively, use curing compounds, described below. Once the concrete has cured, disassemble the forms.

SPECIAL PRODUCTS FOR EFFECTIVE CURING

Curing compounds, generally available from a ready-mix supplier, offer an easy and inexpensive way to ensure proper curing of a concrete slab. White wax-based compounds are visible as you apply them, but may stain the surface; resin-based compounds are less visible, but the dyes fade more completely. Some of these products include a sealer; but if you choose one that does not, wait several months after the slab has cured before applying a sealer, paint, or stain.

Apply the compound when the surface is damp, but free of standing water. To cover a large area, use a portable garden-type sprayer; for small projects, a paint roller works well. Cover the surface completely and apply a second coat at a right angle to the first.

Building a Patio

Patios and play areas are built with the same techniques used for small concrete slabs, such as walkways; but they require a larger quantity of concrete. You can place the concrete all at once or in sections. All the information you need to build forms and pour and finish concrete, as well as the tools and materials required, is found on pages 61 to 79.

LAYOUT AND GRADING

The key to an attractive patio is proper layout. The triangulation method *(page 82)* will ensure square corners. As with a walkway, a patio must slope away from the house *(page 81)*.

TEMPORARY FORMS

To complete a patio in one day, have the concrete delivered by a ready-mix truck *(page 59)*. Even if you are pouring the concrete all at once, divide a large patio into rectangles with forms *(page 84)* so you can level, compact, and screed one section at a time. The center board is then removed and the gap filled.

PERMANENT FORMS

If you prefer to mix your own concrete and pour it in small batches, you can construct a patio with permanent forms that are filled one at a time *(page 87)*. Use decay-resistant wood—cedar, redwood, or pressure-treated lumber—for the forms.

REINFORCEMENT

Not all slabs require reinforcement, but if you plan to surface the slab with brick, tile, or stone, lay wire mesh in the forms before you pour the concrete *(page 85)*.

> ### SAFETY TIP
>
> Put on goggles and a dust mask when mixing concrete. Wear gloves, rubber boots, and goggles when pouring or spreading concrete. Add a hard hat while unrolling wire-mesh reinforcement.

TOOLS	MATERIALS
▪ Tape measure	▪ Stakes
▪ Mason's level	▪ String
▪ Maul	▪ Expansion-joint material
▪ Screwdriver	▪ Gravel
▪ Hammer	▪ Wood screws (No. 8)
▪ Shovel	▪ Wire mesh
▪ Tamper	▪ Pressure-treated 2 x 4s
▪ Lumber for bladed screed	▪ Galvanized common nails (3")
▪ 1 x 12 and 2 x 2 for bull float	▪ Heavy-duty masking tape

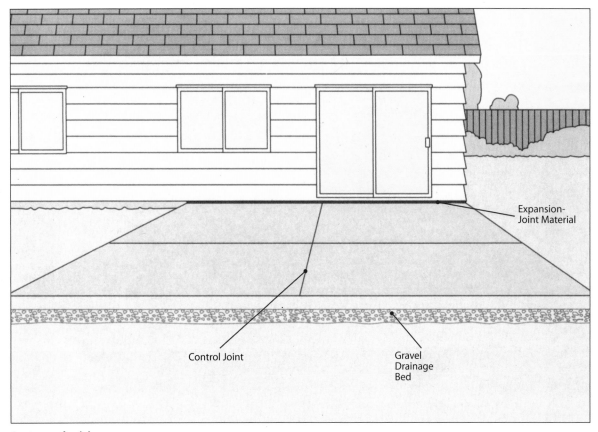

Expansion-Joint Material

Control Joint

Gravel Drainage Bed

Anatomy of a slab

A typical patio has a 4-inch gravel bed topped by 4 inches of concrete. Control joints divide the slab into a maximum of 8-foot squares, and expansion-joint material is placed between the slab and the house. The patio is sloped so that water will drain away from the house.

LAYING OUT THE DESIGN

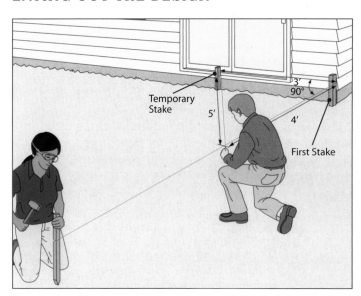

Temporary Stake

First Stake

5'

4'

3'

90°

Marking the sides

Drive a stake next to the house to locate one corner of the patio. Tie a long string to the stake, mark the string at 4 feet, and tie another stake to the string about 1 foot beyond the planned edge of the patio. Drive a temporary stake along the house 3 feet from the first one and attach a string to it. Mark this string at 5 feet. Pull the strings together so the marks meet between the stakes; drive the stake tied to the first string into the ground *(left)*, marking one side of the patio. Remove the temporary stake, locate the second corner of the patio next to the house, and repeat to mark the opposite side.

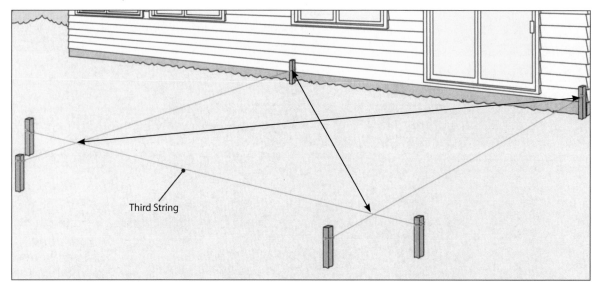

Third String

Completing the layout

Mark the desired length of the patio sides on both strings. Tie a stake to each end of a third string and drive the stakes so the string crosses both length marks. Check that the layout is square by measuring the diagonals between opposite corners *(black arrows)*—they should be equal. If not, adjust the location of the stakes attached to the third string and recheck.

BUILDING THE PATIO

Grading the patio

Following the instructions for a walkway *(page 62)*, transfer the string lines to the ground with sand, excavate the site, and drive support stakes every 3 to 4 feet on three sides of the layout, but not along the house. Mark the corner stakes at ground level, and run strings between the corner stakes, lining up the strings with the marks. Mark the intermediate stakes level with the string. Attach form boards to the stakes *(pages 67–69)*, aligning the tops of the boards with the grading marks. Level and tamp the soil with a vibratory tamper *(below)*.

A VIBRATORY TAMPER

A quick and easy way to compact a large area—such as the soil and gravel for a patio—is with a vibratory tamper, available at tool rental centers. The tool's motor raises and lowers a metal plate at a frequency between 2000 and 6000 vibrations per minute, compacting the surface and, at the same time, pulling the machine forward. The ideal frequency depends on the material being tamped—consult the rental company for the frequency that is suited to your site. For best results, the soil should be slightly moist, but not wet.

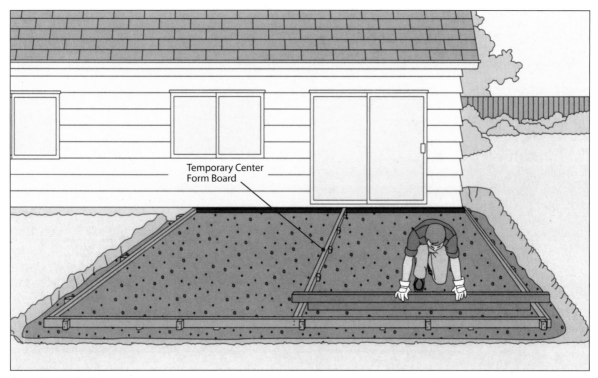

Temporary Center Form Board

Preparing the bed

Place expansion-joint material against the house. Divide a large patio into sections no more than 10 feet wide by setting up temporary stakes and a center form board at a right angle to the house. Lay a gravel bed 4 inches deep and screed one section at a time *(page 70)*, resting the screed on the form boards *(above)*. Tamp the gravel.

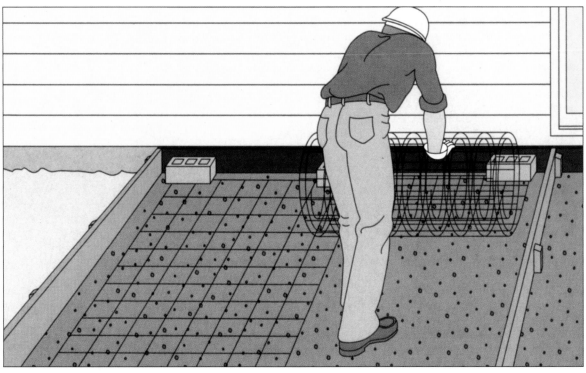

Reinforcing with wire mesh

Start laying wire mesh 2 inches from one corner of the slab section, weighing down the end with concrete blocks. Walk backward, unrolling the mesh, and cut it off 2 inches from the form board at the opposite end of the section. Because the wire will curl, work with a helper to turn the mesh over and flatten it by walking on it. Lay subsequent strips the same way *(above)*, overlapping the mesh by one square. Tie the ends of overlapping strips together with wire. Before pouring the concrete, lift the wire mesh and support it 2 inches above the gravel bed with bricks or stones spaced 2 to 3 feet apart.

CAUTION

Be extremely careful when working with wire mesh—it can spring free and cause injury as it is being unrolled.

Placing the concrete

Pour the concrete, level, and compact it one section at a time *(pages 72–73)*, leaving the center form board in place. Using planks to walk across the slab, remove the temporary center board and stakes, and shovel concrete into the divide *(right)*. Level and compact the concrete along the center with the back of the shovel.

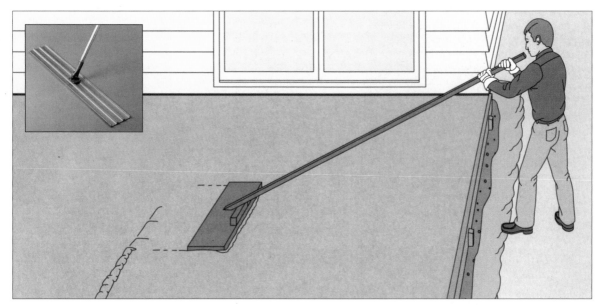

Finishing a large slab with a bull float

Make a bull float, starting with a 12-foot 2-by-2 as a handle; cut one end at an angle of about 10 degrees so the handle will rest flat on the float and the gripping end will be at eye level when the float is used. For the float end, use No. 8 wood screws to fasten a wood block to a 4-foot 1 -by-12, then fasten the handle to both pieces, making sure the screws don't protrude through the bottom of the float. Alternatively, rent a commercial bull float

(photograph). Starting at one corner of the slab, push the float away from you across the surface; push the handle down to raise the leading edge of the float and prevent it from digging into the slab. Then pull the float back toward you with the float flat on the surface *(above)*. Float the slab strip by strip until you reach the opposite end, then repeat from the other side of the slab. Complete the finishing and curing steps described on pages 74 to 77.

KNEEBOARDS TO EXTEND YOUR REACH

An alternative to building or renting a bull float is to use kneeboards made from 1-by-2-foot pieces of ½-inch plywood. Nail a 2-by-2 to each end of the plywood as handles. Work with two kneeboards, reaching as much of the surface as possible from one board and then moving the second one ahead of you. To finish the slab efficiently, alternate between the float and the steel trowel, finishing a section with both tools before moving on. You can use the second tool to support yourself as you lean out.

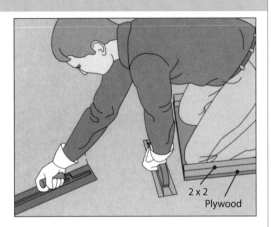

2 x 2
Plywood

A PATIO WITH PERMANENT FORMS

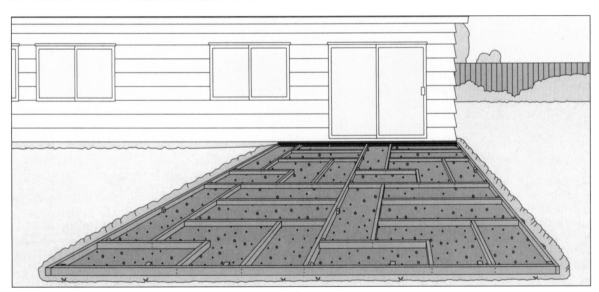

Permanent forms

Forms that can be left in place permit you to divide a large patio into a grid of small sections that can be poured a few at a time—ideal if you wish to mix the concrete yourself and build the patio at your own pace. For the form boards and stakes, use pressure-treated lumber, or redwood or cedar treated with a clear wood sealer. Form boards can be laid out in any rectangular pattern, but sections less than 25 square feet are easiest to manage. For sections longer than 8 feet, cut control joints (page 75) to divide the sections into areas no more than twice as long as they are wide.

Laying out the grid

Place the stakes for the perimeter forms inside the form boards, driving them 2 inches below the tops of the boards. Attach the perimeter forms to the stakes. Lay out the grid for the remaining forms with strings running from the bottom of the perimeter form boards. At each point where strings cross, drive an 8-inch-long 2-by-4 stake down to the level of the string *(right)*.

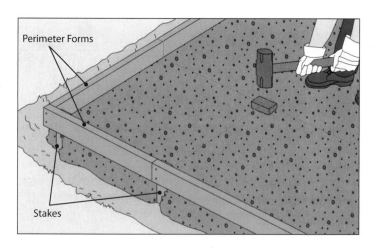

Perimeter Forms

Stakes

Securing forms to the stakes

Rest one form board on a stake and fasten it in place with a 3-inch galvanized common nail driven at an angle. Butt another board against the first and secure it with an angled nail *(left)*, then nail through the first board into the end of the second.

Adding anchor nails

To bind the concrete to the form boards, drive 3-inch galvanized nails into the sides of the perimeter boards midway between the top and bottom at 16-inch intervals. Hold a maul on the outside of the boards to prevent them from moving, and leave about half the nail sticking out. Repeat on the interior form boards, alternating the nail-heads between the back and front of the boards *(right)*. Protect the tops of the boards with heavy-duty masking tape while pouring and finishing the concrete.

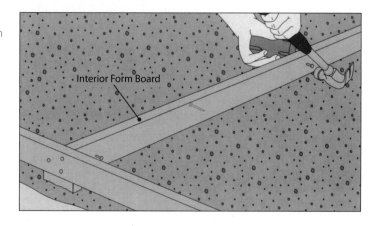

Interior Form Board

A Driveway that Lasts

A concrete driveway may cost more to build than an asphalt one, but the payoff is a longlasting, virtually maintenance-free surface. Although built with nearly the same tools and techniques as a walkway *(pages 61–79),* it requires a curved access at the street; it may also be graded differently. If only cars will use the driveway, a 4-inch slab is sufficient. If heavy vehicles like oil-delivery trucks will drive over it, make the slab 6 inches thick.

PLANNING

For a single-car garage, make the driveway at least 10 feet wide; for a two-car garage, make it 21 feet wide at the garage (21 feet away from the garage, it can begin narrowing to 10 feet). On a scale drawing of the site, plot adjoining features such as the garage, plantings, and house; add the street access and a turning area if you need one. Check local codes for breaking through the sidewalk and curb.

DRAINAGE

Check the codes for drainage requirements. If the garage is higher than the street, slope the driveway as you would a walkway *(page 65).* If the site is level and above the street, it's best to build a crowned driveway—raised 1 inch in the center—so water runs off both sides. But if you want water to drain to one side only, pitch the driveway in that direction as you would for a patio. Where the garage is below street level, make a concave driveway—one that slopes from the sides toward the middle, and install a drain where the driveway meets the garage entrance.

Along its length, slope the driveway no more than 1¾ inches per foot; otherwise, the bottom of the car may scrape against the surface. Make sure the driveway slopes from the sidewalk to the street.

TOOLS
- Tape measure
- Hammer
- Maul
- Shovel
- Tin snips
- 2 x 4 screed
- Darby or magnesium float
- Jointer
- Steel float

MATERIALS
- Stakes
- 1 x 4 or 2 x 4 form boards
- Gravel
- Common nails (½", 3")
- Expansion-joint material
- Flashing metal

SAFETY TIP

Wear a dust mask and goggles when mixing concrete. Protect your eyes with goggles when placing or screeding concrete. Also put on work gloves when working with concrete. When handling concrete directly, switch to rubber gloves.

CASTING A CONCRETE DRIVE

Staking the street access

Lay out and stake the straight part of the driveway as you would a walkway *(page 65)*. Begin the curve of the driveway by first driving a stake at the outside edge of the sidewalk 15 feet from each side of the layout. Drive a nail into the stake's top end, and tie a 15-foot-long string to the nail. Use the end of the string as a guide to mark the curve from driveway to street. Drive a stake every foot from the end of the straight section to the edge of the street.

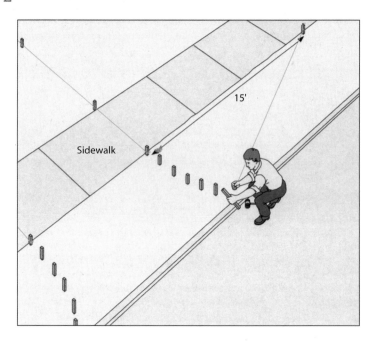

Forms for the street access

For a 4-inch-thick driveway, excavate the site to 8 inches below street level where the driveway will meet the street and 8 inches below the level of the sidewalk. Dig 2 inches deeper for a 6-inch-thick driveway. If you're grading the driveway to drain to one side, use the method on page 66 for sloping a walkway across its width. Set up form boards *(page 69)* out to the street with their top ends level with the sidewalk and their bottom ends level with the street *(left)*. Form the curve with flashing metal cut to the height of the curb plus the thickness of the concrete. Starting flush with the curb, attach the metal to the stakes with ½-inch nails; continue to the sidewalk as shown. Lay a gravel drainage bed *(page 70)* and set expansion-joint material *(page 70)* against both edges of the sidewalk, and against the edge of the street.

Expansion-Joint Material

Expansion-Joint Material

Straight Form

Curved Form

Finishing the street access

Place the concrete (pages 72–73). If you've graded the driveway to drain to one side only, screed the concrete with a straight 2-by-4 (page 73); otherwise, use a curved screed (below). At the street, screed the concrete between the straight boards, then pull out the straight boards. Fill the space at the curved forms with concrete. Shape the sides of the slab at the street with your hands, tapering it from the top of the curb into the driveway's curve and sloping it down to the flat surface of the driveway (left). Smooth this area with a darby or float. Finish the rest of the slab (pages 74–77); you'll need to cut control joints across the width of the driveway and, for driveways over 10 feet wide, up the center. Use a small float and trowel for the edges at the street.

CURVED SCREEDS

To smooth a crowned or concave driveway, make a curved screed: Cut a 2-by-6 and a 2-by-4 to the width of the driveway and place them flat on the ground alongside each other. For a crowned driveway, nail a piece of scrap wood across the center of the boards on both sides. At each end, insert ¾-by-1½-inch shims between the boards so the ends bow out, then nail scrap wood at each end to hold the bow. For a concave drive-way, fasten the ends of the boards together first, place a shim at the center, then secure the center.

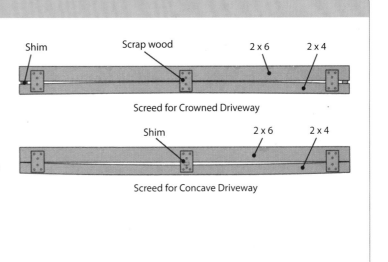

Shim   Scrap wood   2 x 6   2 x 4

Screed for Crowned Driveway

Shim   2 x 6   2 x 4

Screed for Concave Driveway

Sturdy Footings for Strong Walls

Below the base of a garden wall, usually concealed by earth or sod, lies a vital structural element—the footing. This takes the form of a long, narrow, flat-topped concrete slab that supports all the weight of the structure above.

FOOTING DESIGN

Footings for the low freestanding brick, block, and stone walls described in this book do not differ much from an ordinary concrete slab except that they must be built below the frost line on solid, undisturbed soil with no drainage bed. Footings are twice the width of the wall and about 8 inches thick; using 2-by-8 form boards will result in a 7½-inch-thick slab, which is acceptable. Locate the base of the footing at least ¾ inch below the surface; and in freezing climates, 6 inches below the frost line—this is required by code in some areas, and protects the wall

from cracking as the ground freezes and thaws. The wall itself will then start below ground. In very cold climates, consider renting a power trencher, as you may have to excavate as deep as 6 feet. (The illustrations on the following pages represent a footing located just below the surface, in a nonfreezing climate.)

Some local codes, particularly in earthquake areas, require that footings be strengthened with steel reinforcing bars (rebars) to control cracking *(page 94)*. And if the wall itself needs to be reinforced, vertical rebars must be embedded in the freshly cast footing.

BUILDING FORMS

On level ground with firm soil, wooden forms may not be needed: a straight-sided trench will serve. Otherwise, build a simple form as shown below.

TOOLS
- Shovel
- Hammer
- Handsaw
- 2 x 4 screed
- Darby or float

MATERIALS
- Stakes
- 2 x 8 form boards
- 1 x 2s
- Common nails (2½", 3")

SAFETY TIP

Concrete is caustic—wear gloves when working with it. If you are mixing concrete, put on a dust mask and goggles. Protect your eyes with goggles when pouring and screeding concrete, or when nailing or driving in stakes.

Spreader

Building the form

Dig a trench about 2 feet wider than the footing, with the bottom of the trench 6 inches below the frost line. Build forms with stakes and 2-by-8 form boards as described for a concrete walkway (*pages 65–69*), but make the trench and forms absolutely level. Do not follow a sloping grade or introduce a slope for drainage. Fasten 1-by-2 cleats called spreaders across the tops of the form boards every 3 to 4 feet with 2½-inch common nails.

Pouring the concrete

Mix and pour concrete for the footing as you would for an ordinary slab *(pages 71–73)*, making sure that the spaces immediately below the spreaders are completely filled. Remove the spreaders carefully without disturbing the semi-fluid concrete below them. With a straight length of 2-by-4 to serve as a screed, level the concrete flush with the top of the forms *(right)*. Smooth the concrete with a darby or float and cure the concrete *(page 74)*.

A REINFORCED FOOTING

In some areas, codes require footings to be strengthened by rebars; the exact size and number of rebars are specified in the code. Build forms for the footing and, before fastening spreaders across the tops of the forms, run rebars from one end of the forms to the other. These steel rods come in 20-foot lengths, typically ⅜ to ½ inch thick. Wire them to rocks or bricks so that they lie about half of the footing depth above the bottom of the trench. Overlap rebars about 18 inches and fasten them with wire.

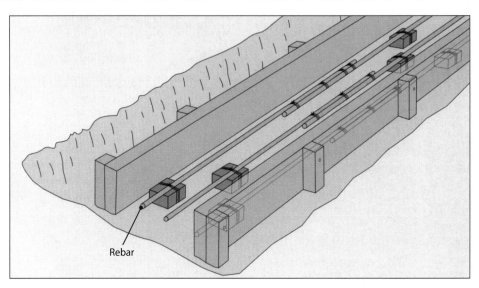

Rebar

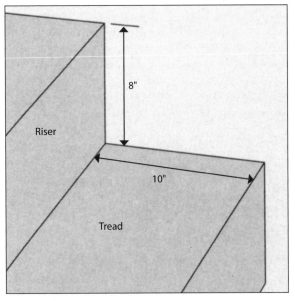

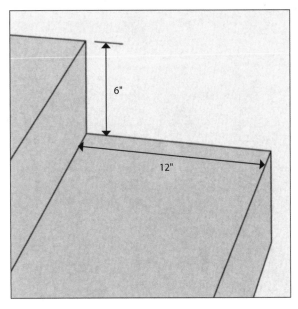

Figuring dimensions

Make the staircase at least 6 inches wider than the door opening. The uppermost step, or landing, should be at least 3 feet deep to provide an area for entering and leaving safely. To find the height of each riser, divide the rise by the number of steps you wish to build. Subtract the riser height from 18 inches to obtain the tread width. Thus, if the rise is 24 inches, you could make three steps, each with an 8-inch riser and 10-inch tread; or, four gentle steps, each with a 6-inch riser and 12-inch tread. From the dimensions you obtain, draw a plan and estimate materials.

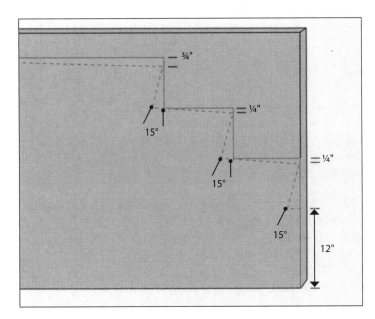

Cutting the form sides

Lay out the sides of the forms on a sheet of ¾-inch plywood, marking the dimensions. Make the height of the forms 12 inches more than the rise, to provide room for 6 inches of concrete and 6 inches of gravel below ground level. Draw risers and treads at right angles with a carpenter's square. Slope the landing and treads downward to provide drainage, pitching them ¼ inch for each horizontal foot; then slope the risers 15 degrees inward (dashed lines). Cut the form with a saber saw, then use it as a template to cut the second one.

Brace

Support

12"

Setting up the form sides

Dig a hole 12 inches deep and about 1 inch larger all around than the steps. Compact the ground with a cast-iron tamper. Nail 2-by-4 supports to the outsides of the form sides with 2-inch common nails. Place the form sides against the sides of the hole, ½ inch away from the house wall, checking with a carpenter's square to make sure they are at right angles to the house, and with a level for plumb. Drive 2-by-4 stakes at an angle at least 8 inches into the ground about 18 inches away from the hole. Nail 2-by-4 braces between the form sides and the stakes with 3½-inch nails. Pour in 6 inches of gravel and tamp it down.

Completing the form

Cut lengths of 2-by-8 or 2-by-10 to the dimensions of the risers. To enable you to reach and smooth the concrete over the entire surface of the tread with a trowel, bevel the bottom edges *(inset)*. Nail the riser boards to the form sides with 2-inch common nails. Cut a piece of asphalt-impregnated expansion-joint material to fit against the house *(left)*. Brush form-release agent onto the inside surfaces of the forms to prevent concrete from sticking to them.

Expansion-Joint Material

Bevel

Placing the concrete

Pour concrete directly into the form, starting at the lowest step *(right)* and overfilling the form slightly; then work your way upward to fill the other steps. If the riser boards bulge out, brace them with 2-by-4s *(inset)*. Drive square shovels into the corners to eliminate air pockets. When the pouring is completed, clear the edges of the forms with a flat spade *(page 73)*. Screed and smooth the steps *(pages 74)*. Once the bleed water has evaporated, finish and cure the concrete *(pages 74–79)*, omitting the control joints. After the concrete has cured, carefully remove the forms. If necessary, patch any chips or holes in the concrete.

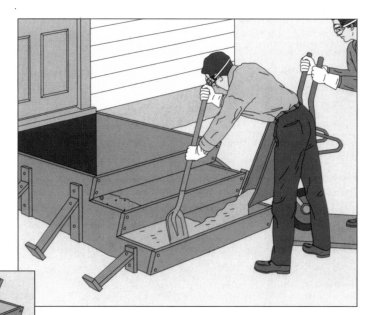

Shaping Concrete into Decorative Blocks

Individual concrete blocks can be made in a variety of shapes for decorative structures such as low walls, garden walkways, and borders for flower beds. Color, pattern, and texture can be added for further visual appeal. These ornamental blocks are poured directly into cavities scooped out of the earth *(opposite)* or cast in removable wooden forms *(page 100)*. The concrete is poured, packed, and leveled in the same way as for a concrete footing *(page 94)*, with some modifications for the type of decorative surface desired. You can mix the concrete yourself in a wheelbarrow or a mortar pan, adding water to premixed concrete or to a basic mix of one part cement, two parts sand, and three parts coarse aggregate.

TEXTURES AND PATTERNS

Forms can be lined with materials such as ridged rubber matting *(page 102)*, although materials with an undercut pattern may interfere with removing the block from the mold. In climates where alternate freezing and thawing occur, avoid surface patterns that will collect rainwater.

Attractive aggregates, such as polished pebbles and marble chips, added to the concrete mix or sprinkled on top of plain concrete, will create striking textures *(page 104)*. Aggregate smaller than ¼ inch in diameter is more versatile for creating texture and pattern. Other decorative looks can be produced with salt crystals *(page 105)*, or by roughening the surface to resemble travertine.

COLOR

Although precolored cement for mixing with concrete is available, it is cheaper to add mineral-oxide pigments yourself—and the color choice is wider. To achieve the clearest colors, work with white cement, white sand, and white aggregate. Mix colored concrete in an automatic mixer to avoid any blotchiness, adding half the usual water until the color is uniform. For a pastel look, the proportions are 1 or 2 pounds of pigment to every 100 pounds of cement; for deep shades, a good ratio is 7 pounds of pigment to every 100 pounds of cement.

Always measure the ingredients by weight rather than volume, and never add more than 10 percent pigment, or it may weaken the concrete. You can make several small test batches; let these miniature blocks cure for about a week, as their color will change slightly in curing. Keep a record of ingredients, so that you can duplicate colors.

The most economical way to apply color is with a mixture called dry-shake—a combination of pigment, cement, and sand that is sprinkled on top of the still-damp concrete block and floated in.

TOOLS	MATERIALS	
■ Shovel	■ 1 x 2s, 2 x 3s, 2 x 4s	■ Form oil
■ Spade		■ Rubber matting
■ Float	■ Plywood (¾")	
■ Handsaw	■ Quarter-round molding	■ Gravel
■ Hammer		■ Polyethylene sheeting
■ Screwdriver	■ Common nails (2", 3½")	■ Wood putty
■ Mason's trowel	■ Finishing nails	■ Pebbles or stones
■ Stiff brush	■ Hinge	■ Rock salt
■ Mason's utility brush	■ Hook-and-eye	■ Mortar mix: Portland cement, sand
■ Nail set	■ Concrete mix	

SAFETY TIP

When mixing, pouring, and leveling concrete, wear gloves and protect your eyes with goggles.

EARTH AND WOOD FORMS

Earth forms for stepping-stones

Dig holes 3 inches deep in the desired shapes of the blocks. Cut the edges of the holes with a spade or a garden trowel so that the perimeters are clean and as near to vertical as possible. Mix concrete and fill one of the holes, then tamp and smooth it with a wood float, leaving a slightly rough but uniform texture; if the stepping-stones are in a lawn that will need to be mowed, make sure their top surface is level with the surrounding earth *(above)*. Pour and finish each of the remaining stepping-stones in this way.

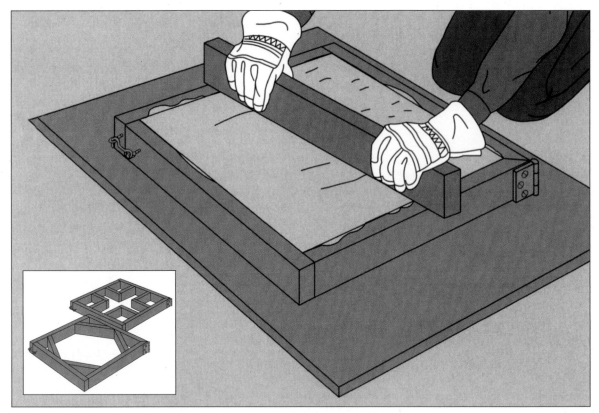

Wood forms

Cut four pieces of smooth 2-by-4 lumber for a frame. Miter and hinge one frame corner, then butt-join the two adjacent corners with 3½-inch common nails; close the fourth with a hook-and-eye. Set the frame on ¾-inch plywood, and coat the plywood and frame lightly with form oil. Fill the form, then tamp and level the concrete with a 2-by-4 *(above)*. Run a mason's trowel between the concrete and the form to compact the edges, then smooth the surface with the trowel. Leaving the block in place on the plywood, remove the frame after 10 minutes, wash it with water, and repeat the process to make more blocks. Let the blocks cure for 24 hours before moving them, then for another six days under plastic. To make interlocking blocks, add removable inserts to a square frame: L-shaped pieces for a cruciform block; mitered corner pieces for a hexagon *(inset)*. For the blocks to fit together, all sides of the form must be the same length.

End Piece   Handle

Ganged forms

Construct a rectangular frame of 2-by-3s with
3½-inch common nails, fastening the end pieces
1 inch in from each end; nail 1-by-2s to the
end pieces with 2-inch nails to make handles.
Install 2-by-3 dividers inside the frame to define
compartments of the desired shapes. Prepare the
area where the blocks will be placed, digging a
trench if desired. Lightly oil the form, and cast
the concrete as you would for an individual
form, but level all the blocks at once by pulling a
2-by-4 over their surface. After at least 15 minutes,
remove the form by lifting it straight up off the
blocks (above). Reposition the form and repeat
the procedure. Let the blocks cure for 24 hours
before moving them, then for another six days
under plastic.

CREATING PATTERNS WITH FORM LINERS

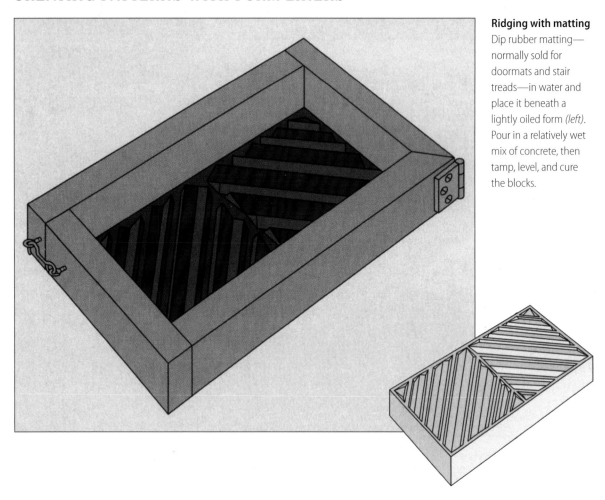

Ridging with matting
Dip rubber matting—normally sold for doormats and stair treads—in water and place it beneath a lightly oiled form *(left)*. Pour in a relatively wet mix of concrete, then tamp, level, and cure the blocks.

Embossing with gravel

Spread gravel of fairly uniform size evenly over an area that matches the internal dimensions of the form, leaving spaces between the individual stones. Lay a sheet of household plastic wrap or polyethylene sheeting loosely over the gravel so that the weight of the concrete will force the film into the spaces. Position a lightly oiled form over the plastic *(left)*, pour in a relatively wet mix of concrete, then finish the concrete *(page 72)*.

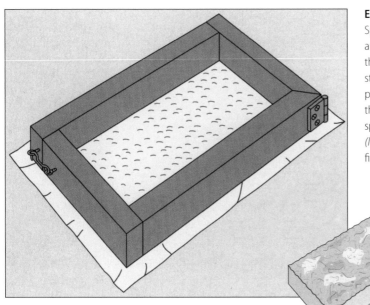

Shaping with molding

Cut quarter-round molding the length of each of the sides of the form, and miter the ends so that they will fit snugly together at the corners. With finishing nails, attach the molding along an inside edge of the frame with the quarter-round facing inward; set the nails in with a nail set and fill in the holes with wood putty. Lightly oil the form and set it on a piece of ¾-inch plywood, also lightly oiled *(right)*. Pour in a relatively wet mix of concrete, then finish it.

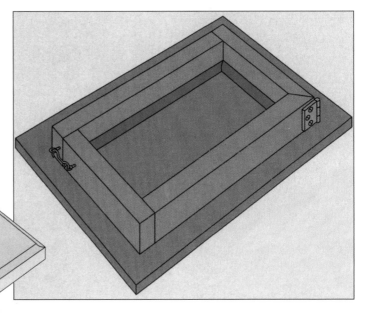

TEXTURING SURFACES

Exposed aggregate

Mix concrete, using the desired decorative aggregate, then pour it into an oiled form. Tamp and level the concrete with a 2-by-4 as you would for a plain block in a wood form *(page 100)* and let it set until the aggregate is firmly anchored but the concrete is still soluble—about 1 hour. With a stiff brush, test a corner of the block to be sure that brushing will not dislodge the aggregate. With a garden hose and the brush, simultaneously flush and scrub the top of the block until the top of the aggregate is exposed *(above)*.

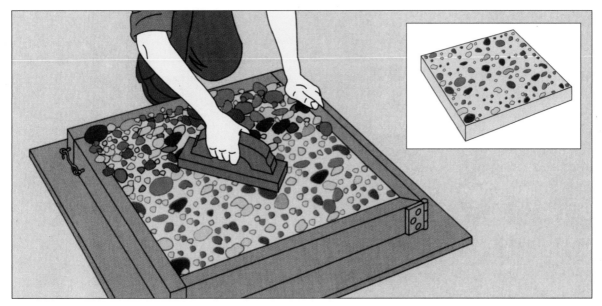

Pebbled paving

Trim a 2-by-4 to the width of the form, then cut a ¼-inch-deep notch at each end so it will fit over the edges of the form. Fill the oiled form with concrete to within ¼ inch of the top, then tamp and level the surface with the 2-by-4. Wet the pebbles or stones to be added, and distribute them in a single layer over the concrete, pressing them into the concrete with a float until they are buried just below the surface *(above)*. When the concrete is set but still soluble, flush and brush the surface as for exposed aggregate to reveal the tops of the pebbles or stones.

A salt-pitted surface

Scatter large grains of rock salt over the block while it is still damp—just after it has been troweled or floated smooth *(right)*. Press the salt crystals into the concrete with a float, but do not bury them. Allow the block to cure, then wash away any undissolved salt with a garden hose.

Making Adobe

Stabilized adobe bricks made of earth, water, and Portland cement are a practical building material wherever the right soil is available. Though impervious to rain showers after a few days, they require at least three weeks of dry weather or protection from rain under plastic to harden properly.

THE RIGHT MIXTURE

Good soil for adobe consists primarily of sand and some clay; earth with a lot of organic matter will not adhere into bricks. You can easily check dirt for suitability *(opposite)*. Make a series of test bricks to determine the right mix of cement and water for your soil *(page 109)*. The ratio of cement to soil ranges from about 10 percent for sandy, gravelly soil to 16 percent for soil with some clay.

MAKING BRICKS

To combine the materials to make the bricks, rent a power mixer, and mold the bricks in wooden forms *(page 100)*. To estimate how much cement you need for a project, multiply the dimensions of the bricks—4 by 10 by 14 is a good size for a first job—by the number you need, and then by the percentage of cement determined right for your soil in the tests. If you plan to build a structure that is subject to building codes, send test bricks to a commercial lab to be checked for strength, absorption, and moisture content.

BUILDING WITH ADOBE

The footing for an adobe structure must extend above ground level. The walls are assembled much like those of standard bricks, and with standard type N mortar, but the mortar joints are thicker—¾ inch.

TOOLS	MATERIALS
▪ Shovel	▪ 1 x 6s
▪ Buckets	▪ Cleats
▪ Awl	▪ Plywood
▪ Wheelbarrow	▪ Common nails (2")
▪ Power mortar mixer	▪ Steel corner braces
▪ Circular saw	▪ Soil
▪ Hammer	▪ Portland cement
▪ 2 x 4 tamper	▪ Polyethylene sheeting
▪ Stiff brush	▪ Plastic pipe (3" diameter)

SAFETY TIP

Gloves protect your hands when working with cement and fresh adobe. Put on goggles when nailing.

ANALYZING SOIL CONTENT

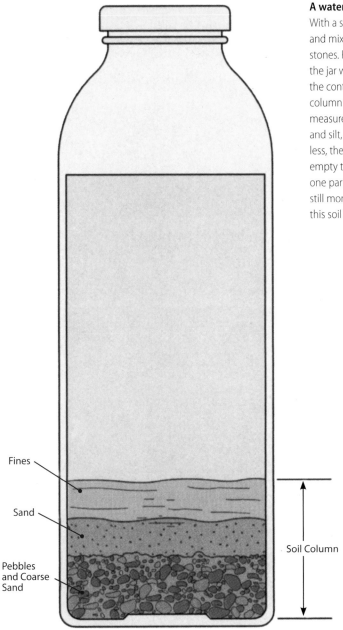

Fines

Sand

Pebbles
and Coarse
Sand

Soil Column

A water test

With a shovel, clear away any topsoil, then break and mix the dirt to be tested, removing any large stones. Place 2 inches of dirt in a quart jar, then fill the jar with water. Cap the jar and shake it until the contents are thoroughly mixed. When the soil column has settled and the water has cleared, measure the depth of the smooth top layer of clay and silt, called fines *(left)*. If this layer is ⅜ inch or less, the soil is suitable. If it is greater than ⅜ inch, empty the jar and repeat the test, but this time mix one part construction sand with three parts soil. If still more sand is required, making adobe bricks from this soil will be too expensive.

CREATING TEST SAMPLES

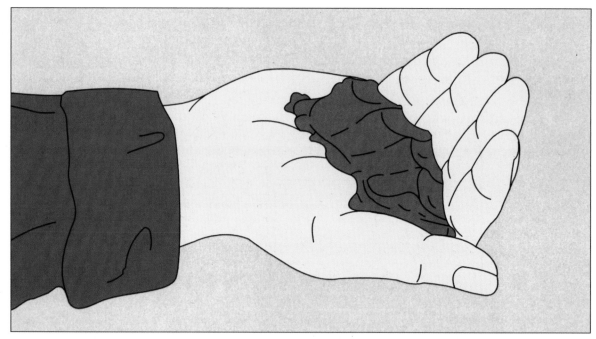

Preparing the samples

Collect several buckets of soil from various points. Measure into a bucket a small amount of soil and cement: If the earth is sandy, use 23½ parts soil and 1½ parts Portland cement. For dirt with some clay, use 22½ parts soil and 2½ parts cement. Noting the amount as you add it, blend in a little water at a time until the mix is moistened. Test a handful of the material by squeezing it firmly, then releasing it *(above)*. If water remains on your hand, discard the mixture and make another with less water; if it does not stay together, add more water—keeping note of how much—and repeat the squeeze test. Form the mixture into a ball and drop it from a height of several feet. If it stays together, discard the sample and mix another with less water; if it shatters, the moisture content is correct. Prepare eight more samples of this mixture, but adding ¼ part more cement to each successive sample and ¼ part less soil. Place one-third of a sample in a container such as a 4-inch length of 3-inch plastic pipe set on a piece of plywood. Tamp the mixture down firmly, then scratch the surface with a fork and add two more layers, tamping, and scratching them between layers. Do the same with the seven remaining samples. Lift off the forms and etch into each cylinder an identification number that represents the cement and water amounts. Put the samples in plastic bags and let them cure for a week.

Testing the adobe

Soak the dried samples in water for four hours. Beginning with the one with the least amount of cement, jab it with a blunt awl or ice pick, first lightly then harder. If the point penetrates more than ⅛ inch but less than ¼ inch, keep the sample. Test the remaining cylinders. From the samples that passed the jab test, knock together two with the lowest amount of cement, gently at first, then harder *(left)*. If you hear a dull thud rather than a clicking sound, at least one piece is not hard enough. Reject the one with the lower cement content, then knock the one the higher amount of cement together with a sample with the next highest amount of cement. Test all the cylinders in this fashion, retaining only the ones that create a clicking sound. If a cylinder breaks or chips—but does not crumble—during the sound test, repeat the jab test on the broken surface. If it passes the second jab test, it is acceptable. Let the good pieces dry overnight, then repeat the tests on them. From the samples that passed all tests, select the one with the lowest amount of cement. Add ½ part cement to the amount used for this sample and subtract ½ part soil to make adobe bricks. (If the bricks will be exposed to foot traffic and weather extremes, add 1 part cement and subtract 1 part soil.)

FORMING BRICKS

Mixing the adobe

The day before you plan to make the bricks, break up any clods of clay in the dirt and mud, and remove any stones. Turn the soil over and mix it, soak it with water, then cover it with polyethylene sheeting. Add water by the bucketful to a mortar mixer, noting the number of buckets, until there are a few inches in the hopper. Keeping track of the amount, add soil to the hopper until it is almost at maximum drum capacity *(right)*. Add the rest of the quantity of water required for the amount of soil being mixed. Run the mixer until all lumps disappear, then slowly add the required amount of Portland cement while the paddles are turning. Keep mixing until the material is uniform in color and texture, then turn off the mixer and double-check the moisture content with the squeeze test *(page 108)*. Make any necessary adjustments, then tilt the hopper with the dump handle, lock it in position, and shovel the mud into a wheelbarrow.

Pump
Handle

Hopper

CAUTION

Do not operate an electric mixer in damp conditions, and cover it when not in use. Never reach into the mixer with your hands or a tool while it is operating. To fuel a gas-powered engine, first turn off the engine and allow it to cool down.

Cleat

Molding the bricks

Rip smooth 1-by-6s to 4½ inches—the bricks will shrink to about 4 inches when they dry—and construct a frame divided into compartments of the desired size; fasten the boards with 2-inch common nails and reinforce them with steel corner braces. Add a wooden cleat to each end to serve as a handle. Wet the form thoroughly and place it on plywood or building paper laid on level ground. Tip the wheelbarrow and shovel the mud into the form, overfilling each compartment slightly; spread and push the mixture into the corners with your hands (left). Tamp the mud down hard with the end of a 2-by-4, then wet the 2-by-4 and pull it over the form edges to level the adobe. Lift off the form immediately, and clean it well with water and a stiff brush. Repeat the molding procedure until you have used up the prepared mud. Allow the bricks to dry flat until they are firm enough to hold their shape—one to four days, depending on air temperature and humidity. Stand the bricks on edge to dry both faces; in six weeks they will be ready for use or storage; store them in rows slightly tilted against a central pillar of flat bricks and cover them with plastic.

CHAPTER 3

Mastering Rugged Materials

Beyond the ability to bind bricks and blocks with mortar, there are a number of skills that identify an accomplished mason. Some are aesthetic—for example, how to select the most appropriate material from the array of choices available. Others are more practical: how to cleave and shape stone, cut or drill into masonry structures, fasten heavy objects to them, and even, on occasion, to demolish them.

Careful planning allows the homeowner to lay bricks and tiles in perfect geometric shapes or in designs that reflect the randomness of nature.

Choosing Bricks

Bricks are ideal building materials—compact and easy to handle yet strong and durable. Available in countless shapes, sizes, colors, and textures, most fit into three categories: building, face, and paving bricks.

VARIETIES OF BRICK

Generally red in color, building bricks are economically priced and suitable for outdoor use. However, they have a less finished appearance than face bricks, which range from white to purplish black, and from rough-textured to glassy-smooth. Face bricks make distinctive walls, steps, and barbecues, but most are not suitable for walkways or patios. There, you will want to use paving bricks, which have one smooth, less absorbent surface, and are shallower (sometimes only ½ inch thick) than other types. Paving bricks come in assorted colors—mostly shades of red—and in a variety of shapes. Precast concrete pavers come in a variety of shapes and can be laid in the same way as paving brick.

Some bricks are solid, and are either flat on all surfaces or have a depression and the manufacturer's imprint on one side. Other bricks have rectangular or round holes, called cores, running through them.

Cored bricks yield stronger walls because some of the mortar runs down into the holes; the tops of walls built with cored bricks must be covered with solid bricks. Paving bricks do not have holes, but you can use cored building bricks for paving where your pattern calls for bricks set on their sides or ends.

WEATHER RESISTANCE

All three types of bricks are rated according to their resistance to frost. Bricks rated SW or SX can withstand severe weather; MW or MX bricks should be used only in climates not subject to freezing temperatures; NW or NX bricks are for indoor use only.

ESTIMATING AND ORDERING

Bricks are usually least costly if you buy them in prepackaged cubes of 500 to 1,000 units. Buying by the cube ensures that all the bricks are about the same color and size.

To estimate how many bricks you will need for a project, first calculate the total area to be covered in square feet. Divide irregular areas into squares or rectangles and add up the areas of the segments. For a double-layer wall, be sure to allow for both layers. Calculate the number of bricks needed per square foot as follows: For unmortared paving, multiply the length by width (in inches) of the brick surface that will be visible; divide the result into 144 for the number of bricks per square foot. For mortared applications, add ½ inch to each dimension of the brick before multiplying, then divide the result into 144. Next multiply the number of square feet by the number of bricks per square foot. Finally, add at least 5 percent for cutting and breakage.

To estimate mortar requirements for paving, figure 8 cubic feet for 100 square feet of bricks. For a double-layer wall, figure about 20 cubic feet of mortar for each 100 square feet of bricks in both layers; for brick-veneered steps, about 12 cubic feet per 100 square feet. A ½-inch-thick mortar bed for paving, walls, or steps requires about 5 cubic feet of mortar for each 100 square feet.

Before the bricks arrive, clear a delivery space close to the street or driveway and as near as possible to the work site. Build a wood platform of boards laid across 2-by-4s for the bricks. Cover the bricks with plastic sheeting.

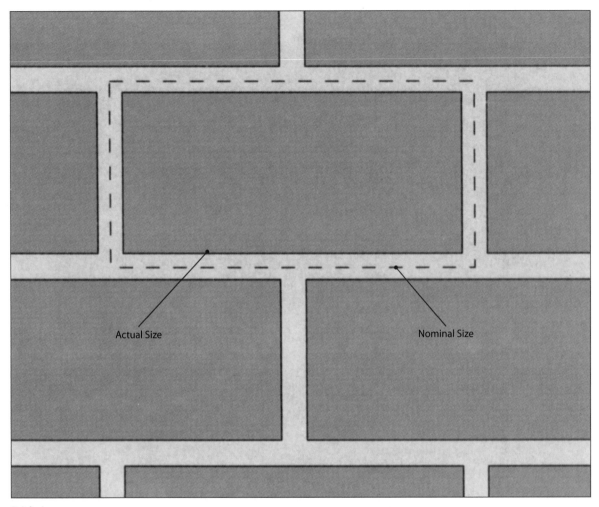

Actual Size

Nominal Size

Brick sizes

Brick dealers and masons sometimes refer to a brick by its nominal rather than its actual size. A brick's nominal size is its dimensions as measured after it has been mortared into a wall, with a ⅜ or ½ inch mortar joint included in the measurement. The standard nominal size of a brick is 8 by 4 by ⅜ inches. The sizes represent only an average, because bricks from the same lot may vary in size as much as 3 percent.

Bricklayers' jargon

The colorful names that masons apply to positions of bricks and arrangements of rows come mainly from terms for brick surfaces. The long sides are called stretchers, the ends headers, and the tops and bottoms beds. When bricks are laid on beds with headers abutting, the stretchers are exposed and the row is a stretcher course. When they are laid on beds with stretchers abutting, the headers are exposed and the row is a header course. Bricks laid on stretchers form a rowlock stretcher course when headers abut, a rowlock header course when beds abut. Bricks laid on headers form a sailor course when stretchers abut, a soldier course when beds abut.

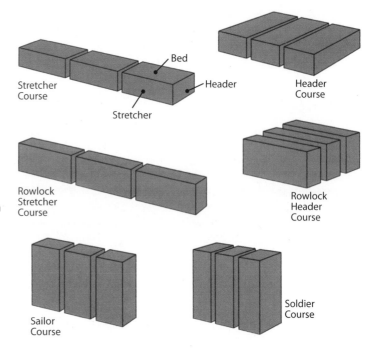

SEVEN STYLES OF FACE BRICK

Bricks are available in a variety of surface colors and textures. Shown here is a sample of common types of face brick. Smooth, wire-cut, rug, and sand-struck textures are created as the brick is formed. Flashing is a method used in the firing of the bricks to add streaks of color. Bricks can be made from a variety of colors of clay; colored coatings can also be added. Tumbled bricks are new bricks given a used appearance.

Bricks For Patios and Walkways

The chief advantages of brick paving are its handsome appearance and ease of construction. Set into a bed of sand or laid in mortar over a concrete foundation, bricks form an attractive and rugged walkway or patio *(pages 148–154)*.

POPULAR PATTERNS

Six classic patterns for laying bricks are shown below. Slight adjustments will yield the variations on page 120. Each pattern requires the same number of bricks for a given area, but laying bricks on edge rather than flat requires 50 percent more. For some patterns, you'll need to cut bricks *(page 28)*.

A plain pattern such as jack-on-jack serves well for small spaces. The more intricate herringbone or basket weave are better for larger areas since several pattern repeats are required before the design is revealed. Bricks for all but the jack-on-jack and running bond patterns must be twice as long as they are wide—nominally for mortar joints; actually if mortarless.

To make sure your pattern choice will work out as you imagined, sketch your walkway or patio area to scale before ordering any bricks. Then cut out miniature paper or cardboard rectangles of the size of your bricks and experiment with different combinations on the drawing.

BASIC PAVING PATTERNS

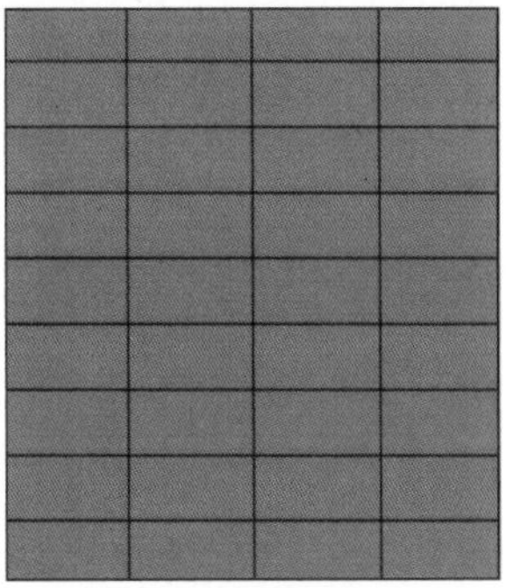

Jack-on-Jack

Running Bond

Basket Weave

Half Basket Weave

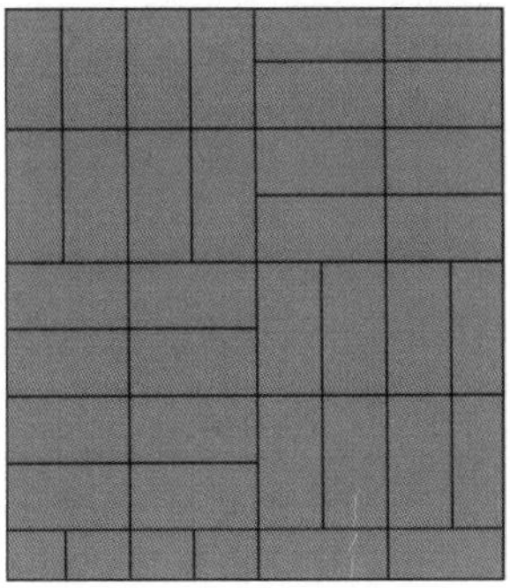

Double Basket Weave

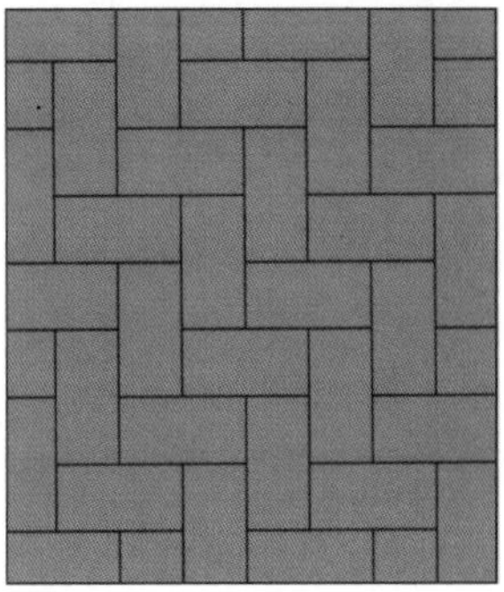

Herringbone

PATTERN VARIATIONS

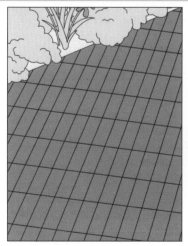

Shifting a pattern diagonally
Arrange your pattern at a diagonal to the edges of your path or patio rather than at right angles. Cut bricks at an angle to fill the ends of each course.

Standing bricks on edge
By setting all the bricks in a pattern on their sides, you get a lighter look than when the bricks are laid flat. To use bricks edgewise in a basket-weave or herringbone pattern, select bricks whose thickness is equal to approximately one-third of their length—$2^2/_3$ by 8 inches, for example.

Shifting the joints
A variation on running bond offsets the ends of bricks in successive rows by one-third or one-quarter the brick length, rather than one-half.

PATTERN VARIATIONS

Changing directions
When two jack-on-jack patterns are set at right angles to each other, a simple pattern becomes more visually compelling.

Combining patterns
For large areas, you can combine two or three patterns. Here, a herringbone alternates with a plain jack-on-jack. Keep in mind that blending two fancy patterns may be distracting.

Gridding patterns
For structural strength, build wood grids into the walkway or patio. The patterns within the grids may be identical *(above)* or contrasting.

Selecting and Shaping Stone

Only a few hand tools are necessary for the relatively simple task of fashioning raw stone into building blocks.

OBTAINING STONE

Most stone used for construction falls into a half-dozen major types *(chart, page 124)*, and comes in two basic forms—as field-stone or as quarried stone. Fieldstone tends to be rounded and weathered. You can buy it from a building-materials supplier or gather it yourself *(pages 129–132)*. Quarried stone has a fresh-cut appearance and is generally easier to split and shape.

Building-materials suppliers often ship in stone from distant sources, and must necessarily raise prices to cover transport. Local stone, therefore, is generally cheaper. Most quarries will deliver it directiy to the building site. You can cut costs by hauling it yourself in a rented truck or trailer.

TOOLS

- Maul
- Stone chisel
- Stone hammer
- Try square
- Pitching tool
- Pointing tool
- Bricklayer's hammer

SAFETY TIP

Whenever cutting or dressing stone, wear leather work gloves, a long-sleeved shirt, and goggles. Hard-toed shoes prevent injury from falling stones.

SHAPING TECHNIQUES

Before starting a cut, study the stone to determine its grain, evidenced by layers or striations, and plan to capitalize on this direction of natural splitting. If the stone has no grain, its cutting characteristics will be affected only by the density of the stone. In general, a dense stone such as granite requires many more chipping blows to achieve a shape than does the less dense slate or sandstone.

Small stones can be hand-held during the shaping process, but place heavier pieces either on a low, sturdy workbench or on the ground. Cushion the bench or ground with padding, sand, or sawdust to absorb the force of the blows. Lack of cushioning may cause the stone to break at the point where it touches the work surface.

TOOLS

The mason's basic shaping tool is a special hammer with a head that is blunt at one end and wedge-shaped at the other. It is used for breaking and splitting large stones or for chipping edges. The best weight for general use is 3 pounds. A maul, blunt at both ends, is used to strike chisels in dressing the face of a stone and to drive the wedge-shaped end of the stone hammer into stubborn splits. Three pounds is also a good all-purpose weight for a maul. Useful for quick, fine shaping of soft stones is a bricklayer's hammer with a chipping blade. The basic set of chisels shown opposite will suit most jobs.

Stone Chisel

Pointing Tool

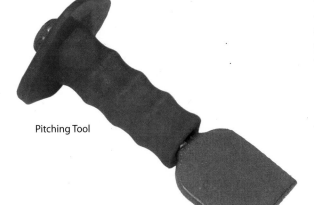

Pitching Tool

Stone chisels

A basic set of chisels for stone work includes a sharp, wide-blade stone chisel for splitting, cutting, and notching; a sharp-tipped pointing tool for fine dressing; and several widths of heavy, blunt-tipped pitching tools for shearing off small protrusions.

A Guide to Common Building Stones

Type	Durability	Workability	Water Resistance	Weight	Color	Texture	Uses
Granite	Good	Difficult	Good	Heavy	Various grays	Fine to coarse	Building
Basalt	Excellent	Difficult	Excellent	Heavy	Black	Fine	Paving
Limestone	Fair	Medium to difficult	Poor	Heavy	Various	Fine to coarse	Building, veneering
Slate	Good	Easy	Excellent	Medium	Purple, gray, green	Fine	Veneering, paving, roofing
Shale	Poor	Easy	Poor	Medium	Various	Fine	Veneering
Sandstone	Fair	Easy to medium	Fair	Light to medium	Various	Fine to coarse	Building, veneering

Selecting stone

This chart compares the properties of several common types of construction stone. Stones in each type can vary greatly, however, depending on the region where they are obtained. Durability and workability are the main factors to consider in choosing a type for a project. A coarse-grained sandstone will crumble, for instance, if it is used for a load-bearing pier or in a wet, exposed location. Dense granite and limestone are suitable for almost any application, but can be difficult to split. If you will be cutting a great deal of stone into thin slabs for paving or veneer, look for a type with parallel grain—natural break lines that will make splitting easier. If your area has severe freezing and thawing, choose a type that is highly water resistant.

SPLITTING STONE

Chiseling with the grain

Position a wide-blade stone chisel in line with the stone's natural grain. Lightly tapping the chisel with a maul, work your way across the stone to cut a shallow groove *(left)*. Return to the starting point and strike the chisel with more force, once again traversing the line. Repeat until the stone splits. If the stone cracks but does not split, you will have to use a stone hammer.

Splitting stone with a stone hammer

Align the wedge-shaped end of a stone hammer along the crack, then strike the flat face of the hammer firmly with a maul *(right)*. Move the stone hammer little by little along the crack, striking it repeatedly until the stone splits apart.

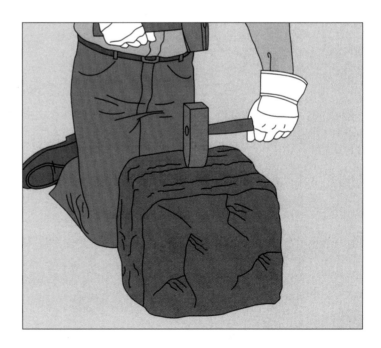

SQUARING THE FACES OF A CORNER STONE

Rough-chipping a flat face

Scribe the cutting line on the stone with the corner of a stone chisel. Turn the stone so the waste edge is facing you. Chip off small pieces from the waste edge by striking the stone with glancing blows from the blunt end of the stone hammer; hold the hammer at a slight angle so that only the edge of the hammer face strikes the stone (right). Continue chipping until you have reduced most of the surface unevenness and are within ½ inch of the cutting line. Check the work occasionally with a try square to be sure the new face is perpendicular to the adjoining faces of the stone.

Smoothing the cut edge

Turn the stone on end. Holding a 2-inch pitching tool at about a 30-degree angle to the face of the stone, strike it with a maul. Continue chiseling in this manner, cutting a little at a time and working from the ends toward the center; turn the stone as required. When only small protrusions remain, remove them with a pointing tool, following the same chiseling technique (left).

BREAKING ACROSS THE GRAIN

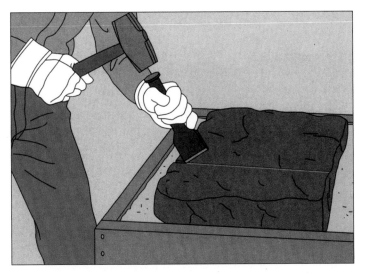

Cutting a groove

Scribe a cutting line on the stone with the corner of a wide-blade stone chisel. Holding the chisel so that only a corner of its blade contacts the stone, tap it lightly with a maul, following the scribed line to cut a shallow groove across the face of the stone *(left)*. Repeat this cut, each time tapping the chisel more firmly, until the depth of the groove is about one fifth of the stone's thickness. Turn the stone over and groove the other face in the same way, lining up the grooves as accurately as possible, then groove each edge.

Snapping off the waste

Align the groove with the edge of the workbench or a sturdy board. Press down on the edge of the stone with your free hand and strike the overhanging waste edge with a stone hammer, bringing the full face of the hammer down sharply against the surface *(above)* until the waste piece breaks off.

Trimming the cut edge

Stand the stone upright, with the cut edge facing you. Remove any large protrusions with a pitching tool and a maul *(opposite, Step 2)*. Working toward the center of the stone, chip away small uneven parts with the chisel end of a bricklayer's hammer by striking across the base of each protrusion *(above)*.

CHIPPING STONE INTO A CURVE

Scoring the curve

Make a template of heavy cardboard cut to the desired curve and place it on the face of the stone. Scribe a cutting line on the stone with the corner of a wide-blade stone chisel, following the cardboard guide *(right)*. Mark the opposite face of the stone in the same manner, aligning the template with the first cutting line at the edges of the stone. Cut grooves along both cutting lines with a wide-blade stone chisel and a maul *(page 127)*.

Removing the waste

Working along the edge of the waste, undercut the stone by chipping out large flakes—about half the thickness of the stone—with the chisel end of a bricklayer's hammer *(left)*. When the entire edge has been undercut in this manner, tap the overhanging edge with a stone hammer to snap it off. Repeat this procedure on the new edge of the waste, continuing to remove the stone in flakes until you reach the groove defining the curve. Smooth the curved edge with a pitching tool and a pointing tool *(page 126)*.

Salvaging Stone

You may be able to gather stone at no cost if you have access to rocky land or a stony creek. Farmers are often happy to be rid of stones plowed from their fields, and the sides of newly graded roads frequently abound in stones unearthed by bulldozers. Abandoned mines and quarries, shown on geological survey maps, may be surrounded by usable stones. Ruined stone chimneys, foundations, and walls also often contain stones of proven utility. Always check with the property owner before collecting such free stone, as it may have been earmarked for another use, or it could have historical value.

GATHERING STONES

The best tool for stone gathering is a 30-pound, 5-foot-long digging bar, available at building-supply houses. It functions primarily as a lever for prying stones from a wall or from the ground *(page 130)*, but can also be used to split large stones.

TOOLS

- Pick
- Shovel
- Digging bar
- 2 x 6 planks for levers
- Wheelbarrow

TRANSPORTING HEAVY LOADS

Because of the sheer weight of stone—one cubic foot of granite may weigh 175 pounds—transporting it calls for some special procedures. If you must haul the stone over a long distance, rent a truck or trailer designed for heavy loads, and take care not to overload the vehicle—doing so may make it difficult to steer. Distribute the stones evenly, and pile partial loads toward the front of the bed.

In preparing to load the stones, drive as close to them as possible. Use a sturdy wheelbarrow to move them to the vehicle, or build an old-fashioned stone boat *(page 132)*. You will need a helper to lift large stones.

SAFETY TIP

A fresh cache of field-stones may hide insects, rodents, or snakes. Wear heavy leather gloves to protect your hands from bites and stings, and from the jagged edges of stones. Put on hard-toed shoes to protect your feet.

EXCAVATING A LARGE FIELDSTONE

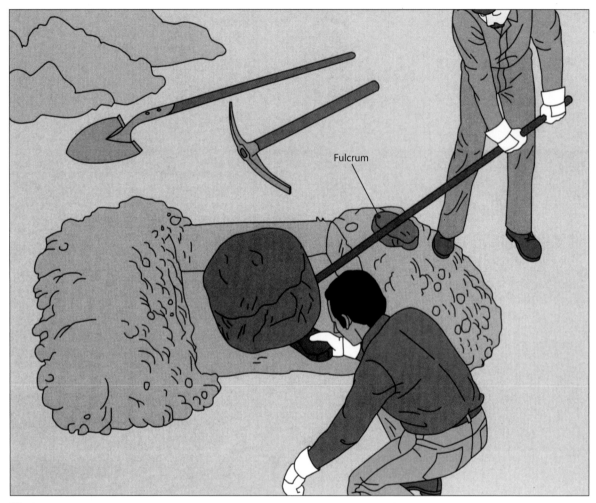

Fulcrum

Digging out a stone

With a pick and a shovel, dig a trench around the stone deep enough to slip a 5-foot digging bar under it, leaving the earth piled beside the trench. Place a sturdy flat rock on top of the pile of earth to act as a fulcrum for the bar. Slide the bar under the stone and push down on the outer end to free the stone, while a helper slips a rock beneath the stone to support it *(above)*. Repeat the levering process on the other side until the stone is completely free and rests on its rock supports.

Removing the Stone

Place a wheelbarrow at the edge of the hole. Slide two long, 2-by-6 planks as far as possible under the stone. Keeping the planks close together and parallel, work the stone onto them by prying and pushing from the opposite side with the digging bar. Bracing the stone with the bar to prevent it from rolling back into the hole, have your helper push down on the outer ends of the planks to lift the stone to ground level *(above)*. From the side opposite the wheelbarrow, slide the bar under the end of the planks to support them while your helper maneuvers the stone along the planks and into the wheelbarrow. When the stone is partway into the wheelbarrow, pull the bar from under the planks and use it to lever the piece into the wheelbarrow.

BUILDING A STONE BOAT

If the terrain is very rough, you can make a heavy sled, or stone boat, to help with the removal of large stones. Design the boat low enough to allow stones to be tumbled rather than lifted onto it. Build it of 2-inch lumber, with removable sides held by metal brackets, and with runners on the bottom, capped with steel strips if possible. Attach a chain or heavy rope at each end to pull the sled or lower it down steep slopes.

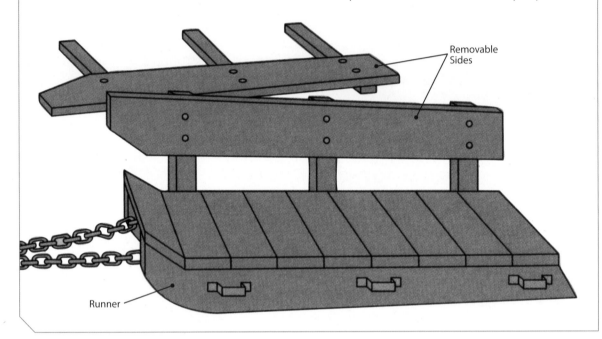

Removable
Sides

Runner

Fasteners for Masonry

When choosing among the many masonry fasteners available, it is important to consider both the load on the fastener and the composition of the masonry itself.

For almost every fastening job there are several suitable fasteners *(page 136)*. The simplest of these are nails, pins, and screws, which are inserted directly into the masonry. Although these fasteners serve for most jobs, they provide only light holding power in soft masonry, and are difficult to drive into hard masonry such as granite or old, dense concrete. For these surfaces, and for mounting heavy loads on any surface, you will need a two-part fastening system.

NAILS, PINS, AND SCREWS

Made of hardened steel, masonry nails can be driven with a heavy hammer. A magnetic nail starter, or punch, steadies nailing in tight places *(page 134)*. Steel pins, with metal washers set behind their points, are a bit lighter than nails but are longer and can penetrate the surface more deeply. Pins are driven with a stud driver, a tool consisting of a protective barrel, which holds the pin, and a piston, which fits into the barrel and rams the pin into the masonry. When the steel pin is fully set, its metal washer will prevent mounted fixtures from working their way loose. For small jobs, a manual stud driver, used with a hammer, serves well enough *(page 135, top)*; but for driving many pins, a powder-actuated stud driver is more efficient *(box, page 135)*.

Masonry screws are often used where hammering could ruin the appearance of a surface. A pilot hole for the screw is drilled first; most manufacturers supply a drill bit with each box of screws to ensure that the hole will be exactly the right size.

TWO-PART FASTENING SYSTEMS

A screw, nail, or bolt fixed in an anchor or shield of plastic or metal provides a solid hold in masonry. The anchor is inserted into a hole drilled in the surface, and the fastener is then driven into the anchor, expanding it to wedge the assembly in place.

Another type of anchor, called a toggle, is used in hollow walls; it consists of a screw or a bolt fitted with a pair of retractable wings that open and grip the inside wall surface when the screw or bolt is tightened.

TOOLS	MATERIALS
■ Nail starter	■ Masonry nails
■ Ball-peen hammer	■ Steel pins
■ Stud driver	
■ Maul	

SAFETY TIP

Wear goggles when driving fasteners into masonry surfaces.

DRIVING NAILS AND PINS

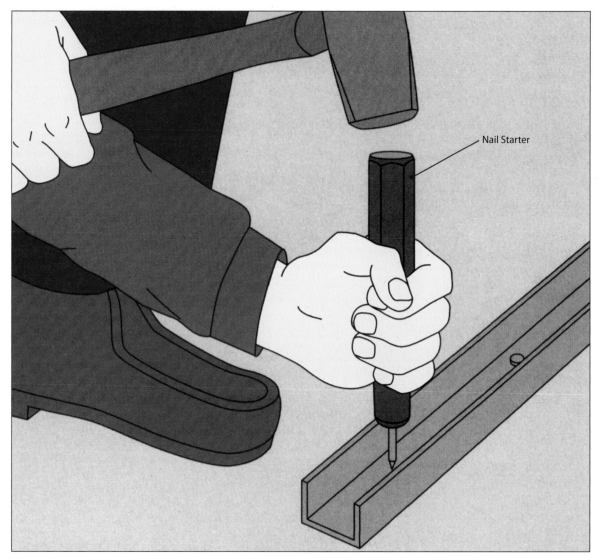

Nail Starter

Nailing in close quarters

Center the head of a masonry nail on the circular, magnetized end of a nail starter, then position the point of the nail against the object being mounted—in this case, a metal channel being fastened to a concrete floor. Tap the end of the nail starter lightly with a maul or a heavy ball-peen hammer to break the masonry surface *(above)*. Drive the nail by striking it with heavier blows.

Washer

Setting a steel pin

Slip the head of a steel pin into the barrel of a stud driver *(above, left)*, pushing the pin into the barrel until the metal washer behind its point touches the end of the barrel. With the pin in place in the stud driver, press the point of the pin against the object being mounted on the masonry—here, a furring strip. Grasp the handgrip of the stud driver firmly and strike the driver piston with a maul, forcing the pin through the washer and into the masonry *(above, right)*.

A POWDER-ACTUATED STUD DRIVER

A quick and easy way to drive steel pins into a masonry surface is with a powder-actuated stud driver. This tool—which is literally a kind of gun—uses the explosive force of a .22-caliber blank to drive the piston against the pin. It must therefore be handled with great care; if you are renting the tool, be sure to get the manufacturer's instructions for the exact model you are renting, as its operation may vary from one model to another. Always wear goggles and earplugs when you are working with the stud driver.

CAUTION

Carefully follow all safety precautions that come with the tool, and read the instructions to determine whether the tool is appropriate for the type of surface you will be fastening into—some materials can shatter or cause the pin to rebound. Keep the tool out of the reach of children.

Suiting the Fastener to the Surface and the Load

Type of Fastener	Installation Method	Adobe	Block, core	Block, solid part	Brick	Concrete,	Concrete, dense	Mortar joints	Stone, hard	Stone, soft
Masonry nail	Choose a nail that will penetrate masonry ½ to ¾ inch. Tap lightly to start; then pound home.				L	L	H	H	L		L
Steel pin	Drive with a stud driver (page 135).				L	L	H	H	L		L
Masonry screw	Drill hole with bit provided. Drive screw through object being mounted and into hole.	L		L	L	L	H	L		
Plastic nail anchor	Drill hole for anchor through object and into wall. Insert anchor and drive nail.	L	L	L	L	L	L	L	L	L
Plastic screw anchor	Drill hole the diameter of anchor. Tap anchor into hole until flush with surface; position object and drive screw.	L	L	L	L	L	L	L	L	L
Metal nail anchor	Drill hole the diameter of anchor through object and into wall. Position object, insert anchor, tap lightly to seat, then drive nail.			L	H	H	H	H	H	L
Lag shield	Drill hole, insert shield, position object, and drive lag screw. In mortar joints, set shield so that it expands against the masonry units.			L	H	H	H	H	H	L
Sleeve anchor	Drill hole the diameter of anchor through object and into masonry. Insert screw or bolt into anchor, tap into hole, and tighten.	H		H	H	H	H	H	H	H
Hammerset anchor	Drill hole the depth and diameter of anchor. Insert anchor until flush with surface, then tap with setting tool to seat. Insert bolt through object and tighten.			H	H	H	H	H	H	H
Plastic toggle	Drill hole to fit folded toggle. Flatten anchor and push into hole. Position object, insert screw, and tighten.		L							
Metal toggle	Drill hole to fit folded toggle. Push bolt through object; and toggle. Insert toggle into hole, pull to hold against inside of wall, tighten bolt.		H							

Application

Choosing a masonry fastener

The chart above shows some of the masonry fasteners available for home use, and explains how each kind is installed. The surfaces for which each kind of fastener is appropriate are indicated on the far right. "H" means that the fastener or anchor is sturdy enough to withstand the pressures of virtually any kind of household structure—including bookshelves and stair handrails—provided the surrounding masonry is sound. "L" indicates that the fastener or anchor should be used for light loads only.

Breaking Up Masonry

Most concrete slabs and masonry walls can be dismantled with perseverance and the proper tools; however, removing a wall that abuts a bearing wall or a slab that adjoins a foundation may have structural implications—consult an architect or an engineer first. Leave dismantling load-bearing walls, reinforced concrete block walls, and cast concrete walls to a professional. Before undertaking any demolition job, call the local building department to determine whether your project is covered by code.

CONCRETE SLABS

For a relatively small job, breaking up concrete can be done with a sledgehammer. Large stretches are more quickly demolished with an electric jack-hammer *(below)*. With either tool, begin at the edge of the slab and work inward. How easily the concrete shatters will depend on its thickness, age, and quality.

Demolition cement is another alternative for breaking up concrete. When mixed with water and poured into pre-drilled holes in the surface, this product expands to fracture the concrete within a few hours. Always follow the manufacturer's instructions for its use.

BRICK, BLOCK, AND STONE

To break up a brick wall with sound mortar joints, chip away at the mortar with a cold chisel and a maul *(page 139)*, working outward from a spot between pilasters, if the wall has them, and from the top down. Walls with old, cracked, or crumbling joints can be more easily toppled with a wrecking bar *(page 140)*. Block and stone walls can be dismantled using the same methods.

If you wish to reuse the masonry units you've removed, you will need to clean them *(page 140)*. Pieces to be remortared in a wall must be fairly flat but need not be entirely clean. Bricks to be laid flat in a patio must be free of mortar chunks; mortar film will wear off with time.

SAFETY TIP

For breaking up masonry, put on goggles and hard-toed shoes. Add hearing protection and a dust mask when using a jackhammer. To work with demolition cement, wear rubber gloves. Use a stepladder or scaffolding to keep your head and shoulders safely above falling debris.

TOOLS

- Jackhammer
- Bull-point bit
- Cold chisel
- Maul
- Bricklayer's hammer
- Wire brush
- Wrecking bar
- Sledgehammer

DEMOLISHING A CONCRETE SLAB

Using a jackhammer

Install a bull-point bit in the jackhammer. Begin at a corner of the slab, positioning the bit against the concrete 1 foot in from both edges *(right)*. Press the trigger on the hammer handle and hold the hammer steady until the bit penetrates the slab to a depth of about 1 inch. Stop the hammer and drill another hole 1 foot in from the edge and 1 foot from the first hole. Chop several more holes in this way. Go over the row of holes you have just chopped several times with the jackhammer, drilling 1 inch deeper each time until you have penetrated the concrete completely. If the concrete does not fracture, reduce the spacing between holes to 6 inches. Continue reducing the spacing until the entire area you have drilled fractures. To break up the rest of the slab, drill holes at the spacing you've determined, working inward from the edge of the slab and never drilling more than 1 inch deep at a time.

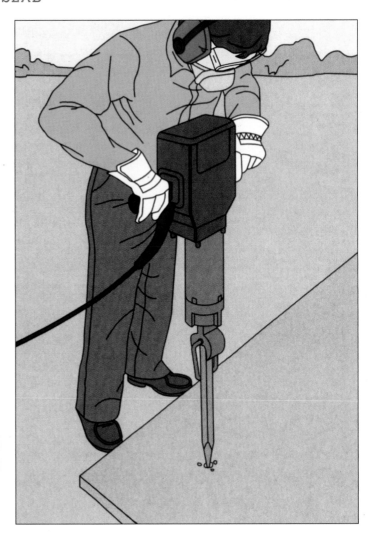

CAUTION

Because of the noise and vibration caused by the electric jackhammer, never work with the tool for more than half an hour at a time.

DISMANTLING A WALL ONE COURSE AT A TIME

Loosening mortar
Starting in the middle of the top course of the wall, use a maul to pound a cold chisel deep into the vertical mortar joints at one end of a brick, driving the chisel into the joint repeatedly until all the mortar has been loosened *(left)*. Knock the loose mortar out of the joint with the chisel point. Repeat the procedure to chip out the mortar from the vertical joint at the other end of the brick. Remove the mortar in the horizontal joint below the brick in the same way.

Removing a loosened brick
Wedge the tip of the chisel into the loosened horizontal joint, angling the point downward. Pressing down on the chisel, pry up the brick. If the brick does not pop out, break it by striking it with the maul and pry it out in pieces, along with the surrounding mortar. Proceed to remove adjacent bricks in this way until the entire course is cleared *(right)*, then follow the same procedure to dismantle the other courses.

Cleaning mortar from a brick

Chip the mortar from the brick with the blade of a bricklayer's hammer *(right)*. When most of the mortar has been removed, scrub the brick thoroughly with a wire brush.

TOPPLING AN ENTIRE SECTION

Dismantling the wall

Force the angled end of a wrecking bar into a cracked or crumbling mortar joint. If you are knocking down a double-thick wall that contains header courses interspersed with the stretcher courses—where bricks are laid crosswise over courses of bricks laid lengthwise—select a mortar joint under a course of header bricks. Push down on the curved end of the wrecking bar to loosen and dislodge the section of wall above *(left)*. If the wrecking bar does not move the bricks, remove it and strike the wall with a sledgehammer to loosen the mortar joints; direct the blows at the wall just above the point where you inserted the wrecking bar. Alternate prying with the wrecking bar and striking with the sledgehammer until the wall topples.

Erecting Scaffolding

Scaffolding made of tubular steel sections that couple and lock together is safe and quick to put up. It can be rented with all the necessary hardware, and many suppliers will deliver the equipment to the job site and pick it up when the work is done. Be sure to get instructions from the rental agency about locking the frame pieces together correctly.

For the structure to be stable, it must be adjusted to the terrain *(page 143)*. Also, very high scaffolding—usually four or more frames tall—must be anchored to the wall to prevent tipping. To determine the anchor height required, measure the length and width of the scaffold, then multiply the smaller of these dimensions by 4. This figure equals the height at which the scaffold must be secured to the wall *(page 144)*.

TOOLS	MATERIALS
■ Mason's level	■ Scaffolding system
■ Electric drill	■ 2 x 10s
■ Masonry bit	■ Masonry anchors
■ Wrench	■ Lag screws (½")
	■ Tie bars
	■ Tie brackets
	■ Tie clamps

SAFETY TIP

Put on a hard hat when working on or around scaffolding.

Anatomy of a masonry scaffold

Scaffolding consists of stackable, tubular-steel end frames held in place by cross braces and locking pins. End frames have footholds for climbing; adjustable jacks in the lowest end frames level the rig. A second level supports a platform for materials. The optional work platform that is clamped to the side of the scaffolding frame brings the mason closer to the rising wall. Planks for both the materials platform and work platform consist of aluminum frames covered with plywood that hook over the end frames. Scaffold-grade 2-by-10s can be used instead, but they must overlap both end frames by 6 to 12 inches. Both platforms have guardrails for safety, and optional toeboards *(page 145)* prevent workers from accidentally kicking bricks or other hazardous objects to the ground. A hoist lifts materials to the top of the scaffold.

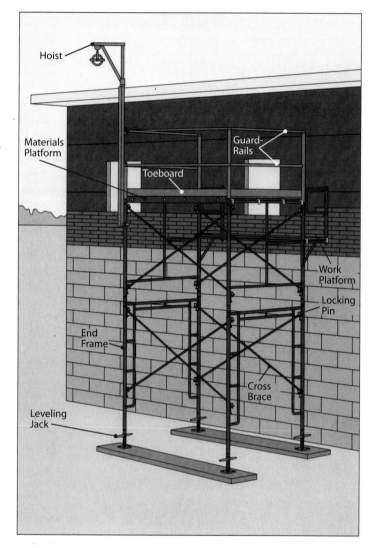

Hoist

Materials Platform

Guard-Rails

Toeboard

Work Platform

Locking Pin

End Frame

Cross Brace

Leveling Jack

STABILIZING A SCAFFOLD

Leveling the base

When one level of scaffolding is together, position the assembly beneath the area where you will be working. Place a 2-by-10 plank lengthwise under each set of legs; on uneven ground, place individual 2-by-10 base pads under the legs. Hold a mason's level against the leg of one end frame while a helper turns the leveling jack until the leg is plumb *(left)*. If the jack cannot be raised high enough, add 2-by-10 pads under that leg. With the level still resting against the frame leg, adjust all of the other legs so that the scaffold is stable and remains plumb. Hold the level across the top of the end frame to check it for horizontal alignment; readjust the legs as necessary. Continue checking and adjusting until the scaffold is both level and plumb. Check it again each time you add a level, and adjust as necessary.

SCAFFOLD SAFETY

✔ Be sure the scaffold is clear of overhead electrical wires. If power lines threaten to interfere with the placement of the scaffolding, ask the local power company if service can be temporarily shut off.

✔ Never use ladders or other makeshift devices to add to the height of the scaffold.

✔ Check all locking pins at end-frame joints and bracing attachments before climbing the scaffold.

✔ Keep both hands on the scaffold as you climb; put on a tool belt to carry tools.

✔ Never jump onto planks or platforms.

✔ Be sure the total load on the scaffold never exceeds the manufacturer's weight limits.

✔ Distribute the load on the platforms evenly.

Tie Bracket

Tie Clamp

Tie Bar

Tying in a high scaffold

At a height four times the narrower base dimension of the scaffold, mark the wall opposite the end frame at one end of the scaffold. For a masonry wall, drill a hole for a masonry anchor to fit a ½-inch lag screw. For wood framing, drill a pilot hole for a ½-inch lag screw long enough to penetrate a wall stud. Fasten a tie bracket to the wall with the lag screw. Attach a tie clamp to the end frame of the scaffold. With the wing nuts provided, join one end of the tie bar to the tie bracket and the other end to the clamp *(above)*. Repeat this procedure to tie the other end of the scaffold to the wall. Where several frames are joined side by side, install an additional tie every 30 feet. Add another set of ties for every 26 feet that the scaffolding rises above the first set.

TOEBOARDS FOR SAFETY

A brick falling from the materials platform can present a potentially fatal danger to workers below. Toeboards, available through the scaffold rental agency, reduce the chance of an accident by providing a fence around the edge of the materials platform. The toeboards, usually metal lengths with interlocking metal plates at each end, are positioned on the inside of the guardrail posts.

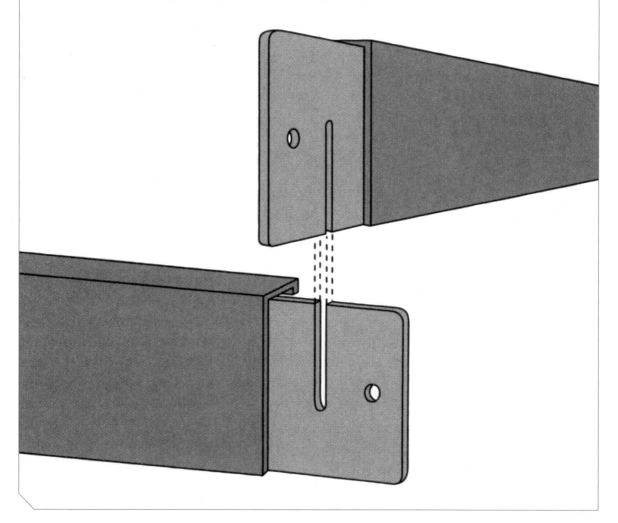

CHAPTER 4

Building with Brick, Block, Tile, and Stone

Whether you are building a concrete-block structure, raising a decorative brick wall, or putting up a masonry arch, planning and accuracy are essential to the success of the project. Even a stone wall, with its seemingly random pattern, requires careful selection of stones and precision in placing them. Beyond standard masonry skills, you will need to use a few special techniques to build these projects.

Whether applied inside or out, thoughtful masonry choices will raise the aesthetic value of your home.

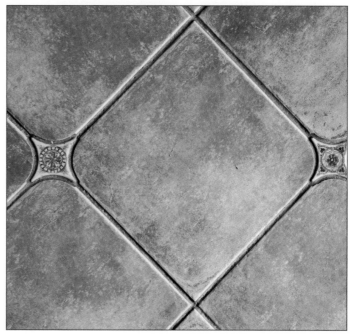

Paving a Path or Patio

A patio or walkway can be built simply by laying paving bricks or concrete pavers unmortared in a bed of sand *(page 119)*; but for a more permanent construction, your best bet is to set the units in mortar over a concrete slab.

UNMORTARED PAVING

Easy to build and with a rustic charm, this style of paving allows you, with a minimum of effort, to salvage the brick later for reuse. In harsh climates, however, the surface may need to be leveled after a few years.

MORTARED PAVING

For this method, bricks rated SX *(page 116)* are laid over a concrete slab. The slab may be an existing sidewalk or patio, or you can pour one yourself using the techniques on pages 83 to 86, making sure to reinforce it with mesh *(page 85)*. As with tile, line up mortar joints with control joints in the slab, cutting bricks as necessary.

EDGINGS

Bricks laid in sand should be enclosed in edging made of brick or of other materials such as wood or concrete *(opposite)*. For a decorative effect, combine wood edging with wood dividers set directly on the paving bed.

TOOLS
- Tape measure
- Maul
- Shovel
- Garden trowel
- Tamper
- 2 × 4 screed
- Mason's level
- Stiff brush
- Joint filler

MATERIALS
- Stakes
- String
- Paving bricks
- Wood strips (1" thick)
- Concrete sand
- Masonry sand
- Edging boards
- Common nails (3")
- Mortar ingredients (Portland cement, masonry sand, hydrated lime)
- 1 × 8, 2 × 4 for screed
- Muriatic acid

SAFETY TIP

Mortar is caustic—wear gloves when working with it and goggles and a dust mask when mixing it. Gloves also protect your hands from the rough edges of bricks, and hard-toed shoes prevent injury from dropped or falling bricks. Put on goggles and rubber gloves to work with muriatic acid.

PLANNING THE LAYOUT

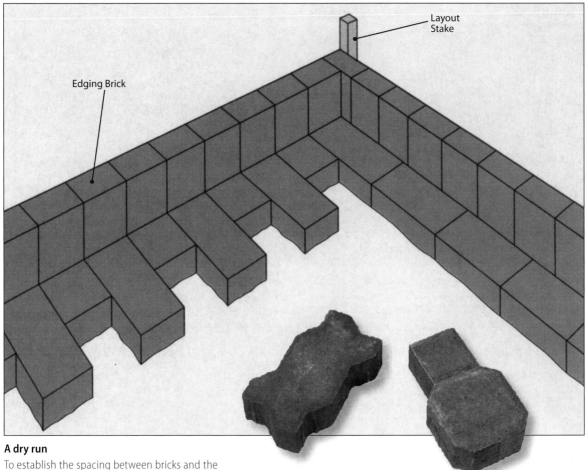

Layout Stake

Edging Brick

A dry run

To establish the spacing between bricks and the dimensions of the paving bed and edging trench to be dug, you need to lay out a dry run of bricks. With stakes and strings, mark the area to be paved as you would for a concrete slab *(page 65)*. Enclose the area with edging bricks set on end up against the strings. Place paving bricks within the edging. For a simple pattern like a running bond, you can save time by laying out the sides and omitting the middle section. If you are using concrete pavers *(photograph)*, place them as you would bricks, following the pattern dictated by their shape.

EDGING VARIATIONS

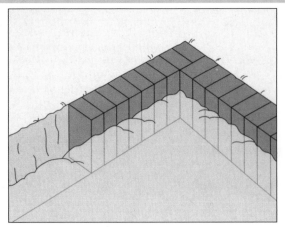

A line of soldiers
The simplest of all brick edgings is a straight sailor course; however, a line of soldiers *(above)* produces a sharper and more attractive contrast with the paving bricks—but uses almost twice as many bricks.

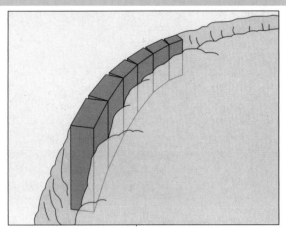

A gentle curve
Curved brick for a curved edging is available, but expensive. You can get the same effect with rectangular bricks by angling sailors to form a gentle curve; then, fill the wedge-shaped gaps between the bricks with soil.

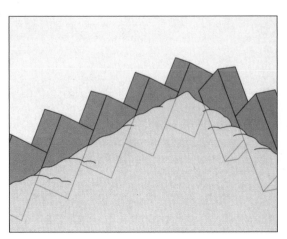

A sawtooth edging
Half-buried sailors tilted at an angle of 45 degrees create the illusion that the edging is a row of triangular bricks neatly cut to size. The brick bases must be supported by packed earth and the tops leveled.

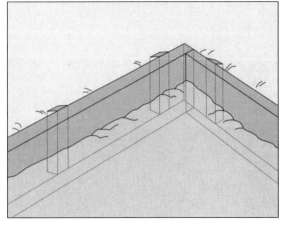

A wood edging
The forms used for pouring concrete *(pages 61–69)* can be readily adapted for edging. Conceal pressure-treated pine or plywood edgings by setting their tops at or slightly below grade and cutting off stakes at an angle. Show off an attractive wood, such as redwood or cedar, by letting ¼ inch or so of the edging and paving bricks project above grade.

LAYING BRICKS IN SAND

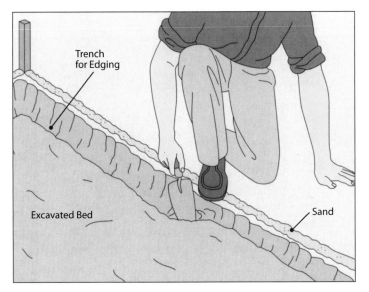

Trench for Edging

Excavated Bed

Sand

Edging the bed

Remove the dry-run bricks and dribble sand over the layout strings *(page 62)* to outline the paving bed. Dig a bed 3½ inches deep, keeping the sides of the bed as vertical as possible. For an edging of sailors, use a garden trowel to dig a trench 2²/₃ inches wide and an additional 4½ inches deep along the sides of the bed *(left)*. Set edging bricks in the trench so they enclose the paving bed with their tops level with the grade. Tamp loose soil up against the bricks to hold them upright.

Preparing the bed

Tamp the paving bed *(page 64)*. For a patio, set two 1-inch-thick wood strips 3 or 4 feet apart along the length of the bed. Pour concrete sand onto the bed between the strips. Smooth the sand by working a 2-by-4 screed across the strips *(right)*. Tamp the sand and screed it again if necessary, then reposition the strips and screed the next section of the bed. To prepare a bed for a path, use the method for screeding gravel for a concrete sidewalk *(page 70)*, leveling the bed so that the bricks will be flush with the edging.

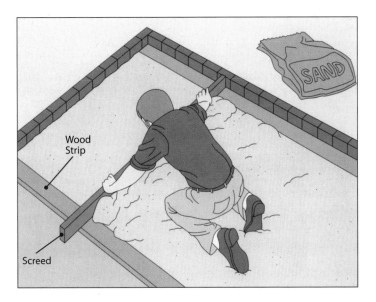

SAND

Wood Strip

Screed

Alignment Brick

Laying the bricks

Work the first two paving bricks into a corner of the bed. To align the courses, wrap a length of string around two bricks; then, position the bricks outside the bed so the string lines up with the inside of the brick forming the first course. Complete the course, butting the bricks together. With a level, keep the tops of the bricks at the same height; tap the bricks lightly with a trowel handle to level them, adding or removing sand from under individual bricks, if necessary. Lay subsequent courses *(above)*, repositioning the alignment bricks to line up the rows.

Filling the cracks

Buy masonry sand and pour a bucket of it onto the bricks. Spread the sand evenly across the surface by hand or with a brush or broom, filling the gaps between the bricks *(right)*. Gently sweep excess sand off the surface, working at a diagonal to the rows. Repeat the process, if necessary, so all gaps are filled.

MORTARING BRICKS ON A CONCRETE SLAB

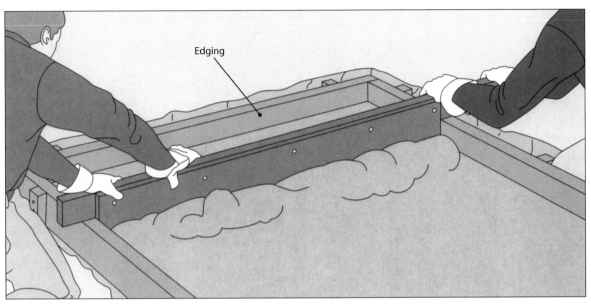

Edging

Screeding the mortar bed

Build temporary wood edgings staked against the outside of the slab as you would build forms for concrete (page 61). The edgings should extend above the slab by the thickness of the bricks plus ½ inch for the mortar bed. Mix a 2-cubic-foot batch of mortar (page 41)—enough to cover 50 square feet of slab. Shovel the mortar onto the slab. Using a screed (page 70) with a blade extending below the top of the edging by the thickness of the bricks, level the mortar (above).

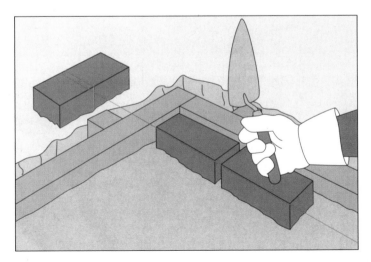

Laying the bricks

Soak the bricks with water. Position alignment bricks using the method on page 154, so that there is a ½-inch space between the bricks and the wood edgings, then set the paving bricks, smooth face up, on the mortar bed. Push each brick into the mortar and tap it lightly with a trowel handle (left). Use a wood scrap to space the bricks ½ inch apart and a level to keep their tops flush with top of the edging. For a small area, lay one complete course across the slab before starting the next; for a large one, lay rectangular segments of about 4 by 8 feet.

Edging the slab

For a slab above grade, remove the wood edging to make room for edging bricks to conceal the concrete and shield the paving bricks from damage and moisture. Enlarge the trench around the slab to about 2½ inches wide and deep enough to accommodate a 2-inch layer of mortar so the tops of the edging bricks will be flush with the paving bricks. Trowel a layer of mortar 3 to 4 inches deep along the trench. Soak the edging bricks and embed them in the mortar in the trench ½ inch apart as sailors, flat faces out *(right)*; the excess mortar will be squeezed up around the bricks. With a level, check that the bricks are flush with the paving bricks. Tamp soil against the outside of the edging bricks to pin them to the slab.

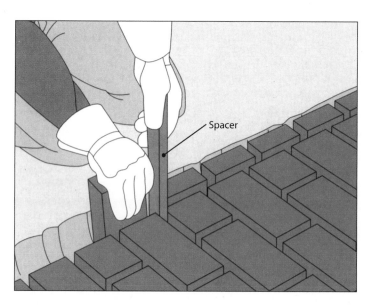

Spacer

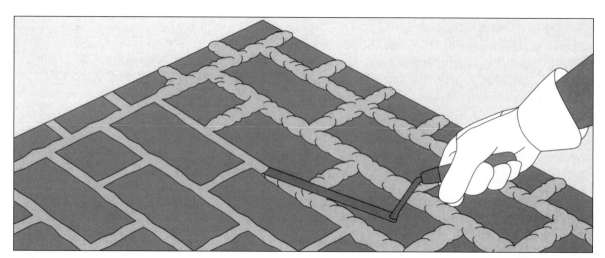

Grouting the joints

At least one day after laying the bricks, prepare a batch of mortar *(page 42)*. Hose down the bricks. Lay ridges of mortar on the joints and work it in with a joint filler or pointing trowel, tamping it firmly and overfilling the joints slightly. After about an hour—but before the mortar has fully hardened—remove any excess from the joints with the edge of the joint filler or trowel *(above)*. When the mortar is thumbprint hard, finish the joints with a ¾-inch convex jointer *(pages 19–21)*. After another three hours, smooth the joints with a stiff brush or a small sand-filled burlap bag. Brush mortar from the bricks and hose them down thoroughly. When the mortar has set completely—in about two days—remove any dried mortar with muriatic acid solution, adding 1 part acid to 10 parts water (or 15 parts water for light-colored brick).

CAUTION

Always pour acid into water, never water into acid.

Building a Brick Wall

A freestanding wall can lend charm to a yard, enclosing spaces such as flower beds and play areas. The simplest wall to build is straight *(pages 158–164)*; a wall with corners has a few variations *(pages 167–169)*.

CHOOSING THE SITE

Start by consulting local ordinances, building codes, and your neighbors to ensure there are no legal obstacles to your plans. Next, check the soil for drainage; even a well-erected wall may buckle or sink on marshy or spongy ground. Examine the site carefully—hills and slopes present special difficulties. Avoid large trees with thick and widespread roots; and make sure that the concrete footing *(pages 92–94)*, which will be twice the width of the wall, will not encroach on an adjacent property line or sidewalk.

BUILDING THE WALL

There are several different ways of arranging the bricks, but running bond is the simplest. Walls shorter than 3 feet generally do not require reinforcing *(page 158)*, but in some areas, you can build a wall up to 5 or 6 feet high without reinforcement—check local codes.

TOOLS	MATERIALS
■ Tape measure	■ Lumber for story pole
■ Maul	■ Stakes
■ Brick set	■ String
■ Ball-peen hammer	■ Bricks
■ Shovel	■ 2 × 8 form boards
■ Hammer	■ Common nails (3")
■ Chalk line	■ Concrete
■ Mason's trowel	■ Mortar ingredients (Portland cement, masonry sand, lime)
■ Mason's level	
■ Mason's line	■ Wall ties
■ Line twigs and pins	■ Rebars
■ Jointer	■ 1 × 6s
■ Carpenter's square	■ Sand
■ Plumb bob	

SAFETY TIP

Mortar is caustic—wear gloves when working with it; add goggles and a dust mask when mixing it. Gloves also protect your hands from the rough edges of bricks, and hard-toed shoes prevent injury from dropped or falling brick.

A STORY POLE FOR SPACING BRICKS

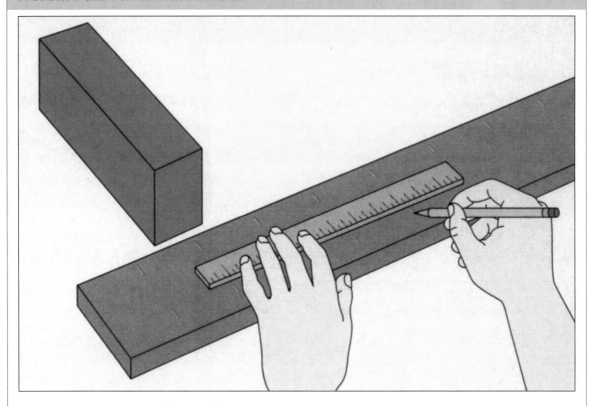

To keep the courses of a brick wall on track, use a homemade measuring stick called a story pole. Cut a piece of scrap lumber to the planned height of the wall. With an indelible marker, draw a line near one end of the pole at the height of the top of the bricks in the first course; allow for a ½-inch mortar bed plus the actual height of a brick *(page 20)*. Add a mark for each successive course to the opposite end of the pole. As you build the wall, set the pole against the newly laid bricks to make sure that the courses rise evenly.

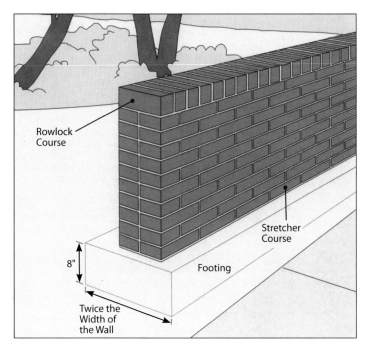

Rowlock Course

Stretcher Course

Footing

8"

Twice the Width of the Wall

Anatomy of a brick wall

A freestanding brick wall rests on a footing *(pages 92–94)*—a cast concrete slab 8 inches thick and twice as wide as the wall. The bottom of the footing must be 6 inches below the frost line. (The footing shown here is just below the surface as it would be in a frost-free area.) In areas with a deep frost line, you may want to build the part of the wall that is below grade from inexpensive concrete blocks. For strength, the wall shown on these pages has two parallel layers, separated by a narrow air space, which is mortared only at the ends. The layers are bound together at regular intervals by metal strips called wall ties. The ties are placed atop every other course, starting with the second. Both layers are laid as stretcher courses, with ½-inch-thick vertical and horizontal mortar joints. The wall is capped by a rowlock course extending from the front of the wall to the back.

PLANNING THE LAYOUT

A dry run for the first courses

From a horizontal reference line, such as the side of your house or property line, measure to the baseline you have chosen for the front of the wall. Drive stakes at the ends of this line and stretch a string between them. Lay the face course of bricks, following the string and spacing the bricks with a ½-inch wood scrap. Place the rear, or backup, course of bricks ½ inch behind the face course, starting with a half brick *(page 28)* and continuing with full-length stretchers. Every few bricks, set a rowlock brick crosswise *(right)*; if it is not flush with the outside edges of the front and back bricks, adjust the space between them; measure and note this distance. Finish laying the courses, ending the rear course with a half brick. Adjust the stakes to the length of the wall and measure its length.

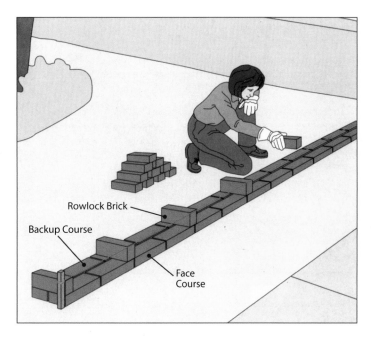

Rowlock Brick

Backup Course

Face Course

PREPARING THE FOOTING

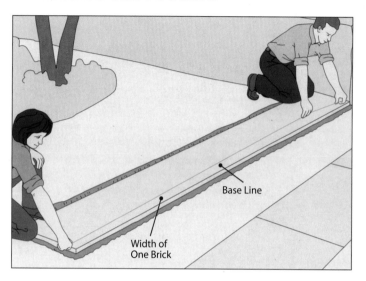

Base Line

Width of
One Brick

Building and marking the footing

Mark the baseline for the wall on the ground with stakes, string, and sand *(page 63)*. From this reference point, mark and dig a trench for the footing so the footing will be 8 inches (two brick widths) wider than the wall and its front edge will be offset from the front of the wall by 4 inches (one brick width). Assemble the forms and pour the concrete following the directions on pages 92 to 94. If the wall will be more than 3 to 6 feet high, add reinforcement *(below)*. With a chalk line, mark the wall's baseline on the footing *(left)*. Mark both ends of the wall on the footing, using the measurement you took after making the dry run *(page 159)*.

REINFORCING A HIGH WALL

To conform to building codes, walls over a certain height must be strengthened with steel reinforcing bars (rebars). Local codes determine the minimum height of such a wall—generally 3 to 6 feet—as well as the exact diameter and spacing of the rebars. Cast into the footing when it is poured, the first rebars extend about a foot above the slab. As the wall is built up, additional bars are tied to these with wire so the rods overlap by an amount specified by code. Once the wall is completed, the space between the face and backup courses is filled with mortar.

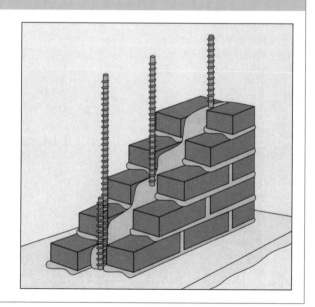

CONSTRUCTING THE LEADS

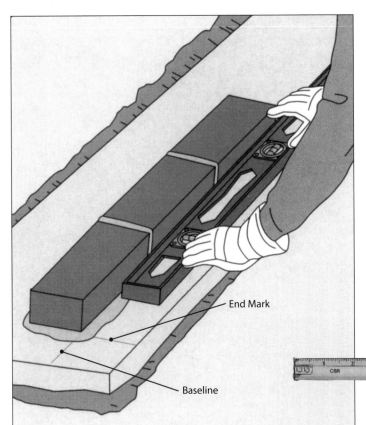

End Mark

Baseline

Laying the first bricks

Soak the bricks before laying them. Mix about 2 cubic feet of mortar *(page 16)*. Moisten 3 feet of the footing surface at one end with a fine spray of water. Let the excess water evaporate. Throw a mortar line just behind the chalk line and, starting at the end mark, lay up three bricks on the mortar bed *(pages 18–21)*. Make all mortar joints ½ inch thick. To align the bricks with the baseline, hold a level or straightedge against the bricks *(left)* and adjust their position if necessary. Set your story pole *(page 158)* against the bricks at various points—the top of the brick should align with the first mark on the pole. Or, use a brick-spacing tape to check height *(photograph)*. Tap down on any brick that is too high; if bricks are too low, remove them and throw a new mortar bed.

Starting the backup course

Throw a mortar line about ½ inch behind the front bricks. Spread a little mortar on the edge of a half brick at the outside end—this will seal the air gap between the face and backup courses at the ends of the wall. Position the brick at the end mark, spacing it from the face course by the measured amount. Continue the backup course with two stretcher bricks. (As the wall rises, half bricks will alternate between the ends of the face and backup courses.) Align the backup bricks with a level and check that the front and back bricks are level with each other. Start the second courses of face and backup bricks, beginning with a half brick for the face course and a whole brick for the backup. Lay two whole bricks on the face course and one on the backup course so there is a step up from the first to second course. Check the course heights with the story pole *(right)*.

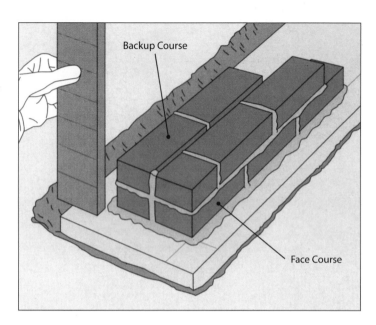

Placing wall ties

Throw a mortar line on the second face course and embed ties in the mortar about 12 inches apart with the free ends of the ties lying over the backup course *(left)*. Lay two whole stretcher bricks of the third face course over the ties.

Mortaring the ties

Once the mortar under the third face course has begun to set, bend the wall ties up away from the backup bricks, being careful not to displace any units. Throw a mortar line on the backup bricks, then bend the ties down into the mortar *(top, left)*. Start the third backup course—a half brick followed by a whole one.

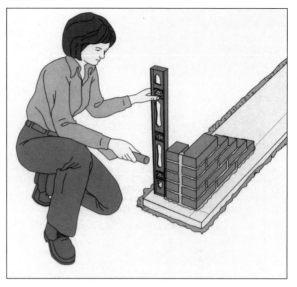

Completing the first lead

Lay five face and backup courses, adding wall ties between the fourth and fifth courses. Complete the lead—the end of the wall—by placing a single brick at the end of the face course and a half brick at the end of the backup. Check with a level or straightedge for vertical alignment. Ignoring minor irregularities, gently tap any protruding brick with a trowel handle to push it into line *(top, right)*. Tap a recessed brick into line from behind.

Building the opposite lead

At the opposite end of the footing, repeat these Steps to form a five-course lead. Check carefully with the story pole and the level *(left)*—unless the two leads match exactly, the wall will be unstable.

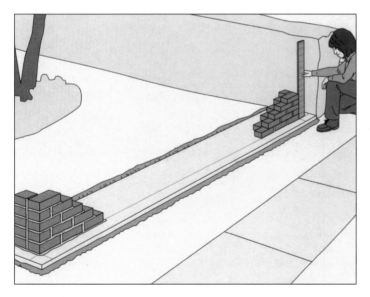

FILLING IN BETWEEN THE LEADS

A mason's line for aligning courses

Tie a mason's line to a mason's block, feeding the free end of the line through the slot. Hook the block around one end brick in the first face course, aligning the string with the top of the brick. Extend the line to the other end of the wall and feed the line through the slot of another mason's block. Pull the line taut and wrap it around the block. Hook the second block around the end brick in the first course, keeping the string flush with the top edge of the brick *(right)*. Set up a second line along the rear course. On a long wall, use a mason's tool called a line twig to support the string near the middle *(inset)*; at the center of the run, lay a brick on a piece of plywood as thick as the mortar joints, position the line twig on the brick, then set a second brick on top to hold it in place.

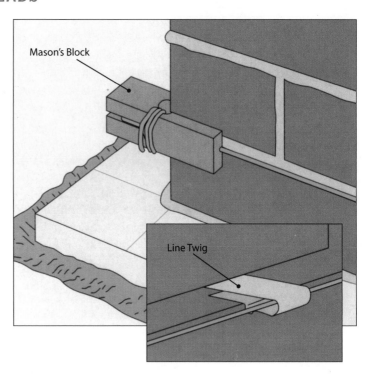

Mason's Block

Line Twig

Laying bricks between the leads

Working from the ends of the wall toward the middle, complete the first face course, using the mason's line as a guide. At the center of the course, place a closure brick, buttering both ends with mortar *(page 21)*. Finish laying the first backup course the same way.

Mason's Line

Building to the top of the leads

Working from the ends toward the middle of the wall, finish the next four face and backup courses *(left)*. Move the mason's line up one course at a time as you proceed and insert wall ties atop the second and fourth courses *(page 162–163)*. If the wall will stop at this height, add a rowlock course *(page 166)* and finish the joints *(page 22)*; for a taller wall, proceed as below.

Extending the wall upward

Add reinforcement bars as necessary *(page 160)*; then, build new five-course leads at the ends and fill in the courses between the leads, always working from the ends toward the middle. Use a story pole as a guideline for the leads *(page 158)* and a mason's line for the bricks between them *(right)*.

CAPPING THE WALL

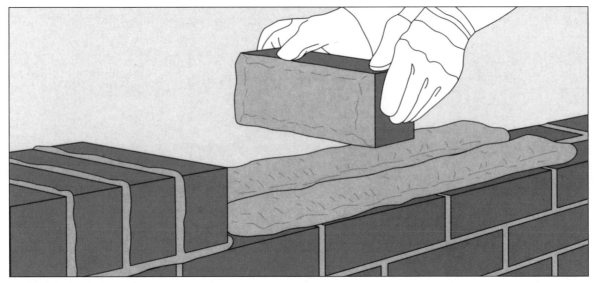

Laying the rowlocks

Starting at one end of the wall, throw mortar lines on the top face and backup course. Set the first rowlock brick at the end of the wall. Butter one side of the next brick, and lay it alongside the first with a ½-inch joint between bricks. Lay rowlocks to the end of the wall. With standard-size bricks, every third joint in the rowlocks should align with a joint in the course below *(above)*. If not, stop laying rowlocks and lay a dry run from that point on as shown below before finishing the cap. Finish the joints in the rowlock course *(page 22)*.

A dry run

Before throwing any more mortar, lay rowlocks to the end of the wall. Adjust the joint spacing so that the last brick rests flush with the end of the wall *(left)*. With a pencil, mark the brick locations on the wall. Remove the bricks and complete the rowlock course as described above, aligning each brick with its marks on the wall.

BUILDING A WALL WITH CORNERS

Planning the wall

Outside the corners of the proposed wall,
set up four L-shaped sets of boards—called
batter boards—each built from two 1-by-6s or
1-by-8s nailed to three stakes. Set up a string guide
for the most prominent wall (Wall A in this case)
and tie it to a nail in the batter board. Make a dry
run of the face course of Wall A as for any straight
wall *(page 159)*. Lay out the corners by setting
single bricks at right angles to the ends of Wall A.
Check for square with a carpenter's square. Set up
string guides for Walls B and C. With a plumb bob,
check that the intersection of the strings is directly
above the corners of the wall. Use the triangulation
method *(page 82)* to make sure the strings cross at
exactly 90 degrees. Lay a dry run for Walls B and C
(right). With a plumb bob, mark the string at the
end of these sections. Add string lines to the batter
boards one brick width to each side of the wall
to locate footings *(dashed lines)*. Transfer the lines

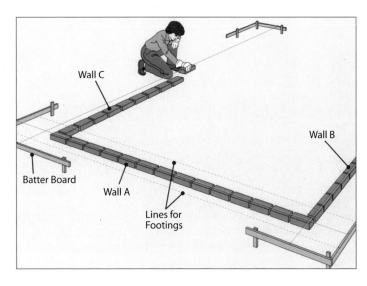

for the footings to the ground with sand *(page 62)*.
Remove the strings, leaving the batter boards in
place. Mark the string locations.

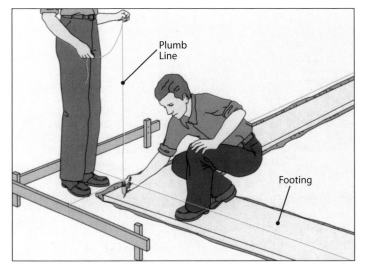

Marking the walls

Dig a trench, build forms, and pour concrete for each
footing following the method on pages 92 to 94.
If the wall will be more than 3 to 6 feet high, add
reinforcement *(page 160)*. Retie the batter board
strings for the front faces of the walls. Drop a plumb
bob to mark the corners *(left)* and ends of the wall
on the footings. On each footing, snap a chalk line
between these marks to locate the face course
of bricks *(page 160)*. Remove the batter boards
and strings.

Forming the corner

Throw two mortar lines at one corner of the wall just inside the chalk lines using the technique on page 19. Lay brick A at the corner, then butter and lay brick B, using a carpenter's square to check that the bricks form a right angle. Lay the next four bricks in order—C, D, E, and F—making a six-brick corner lead. With a level or straightedge, check that the bricks are flush with the chalk lines *(right)*.

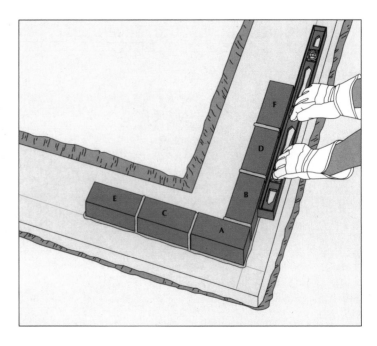

Starting the backup lead

Throw mortar lines behind the face course, and lay the first three bricks of the backup course spacing them ½ inch away from the face bricks to accommodate a course of rowlocks on top of the wall, as illustrated on page 166. Check that the backup bricks form a right angle and are offset from the face bricks by a half brick *(left)*. Verify the height of the courses with the story pole *(page 158)*.

Backup Course

Face Course

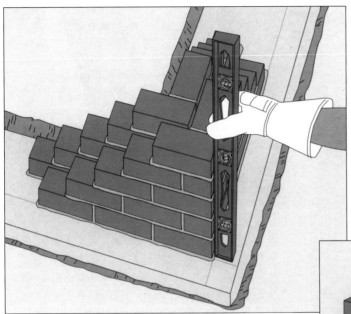

Completing the leads

Working on both the front and backup courses, build up the corner lead to a height of five courses, checking the alignment of the bricks *(left)*. In the same manner, build the other corner and end leads. Stretch a mason's line between the corners and fill in between the leads, adapting the techniques on pages 164 to 165. On the inside of the wall, drive line pins into mortar joints to anchor the mason's line *(inset)*. If the wall will be higher than five courses, add reinforcement *(page 160)*, then add new corner and end leads, and lay bricks between them until you reach the desired height.

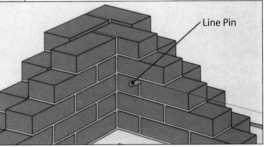

Line Pin

Laying the rowlocks

Add rowlocks for one wall as you would for a straight wall *(page 166)*. Lay the rowlocks for the adjoining walls so the bricks meet at the corners at right angles, as shown at left.

Veneering a Concrete Slab with Tile

An elegant way to finish a walkway or patio is with tiles. Illustrated here are ceramic tiles, but tiles made of stone, such as marble or slate, are laid in the same way.

WHAT TO BUY

Ceramic tiles suited for outdoor use are paver and quarry tile, which are 6, 8, or 12 inches square and about ⅜ inch thick. The top edges of pavers are slightly rounded, while those of quarries are square edged. Buy only unglazed tiles—glazed tile will be slippery underfoot. Consult your supplier to ensure that you buy tiles suitable for your climate; or plan on sealing the tiles to prevent them from absorbing water, which can freeze in winter and crack the tiles.

To lay down the mortar bed for the tiles, you'll need a notched quarry-tile trowel—ask your tile supplier what notch size is appropriate for the tiles you buy.

PREPARING THE SLAB

Tiles should not overlap the control joints in the slab. If you are casting a new slab *(pages 80–88)*, you can size it to accommodate an even number of tiles and to ensure that they line up with the control joints. This will prevent your having to cut the tiles to fit. An uneven base will cause the tiles to tilt or even crack; before laying tiles, check and, if necessary, smooth the surface.

MAKING A DRY RUN

To determine the exact spacing of tiles, lay out a dry run along two adjacent edges of the slab. If the tiles have lugs—built-in spacers projecting from the edges—simply place them with the lugs touching. For tiles lacking lugs, lay them ⅜ inch apart using a spacer. When tiles fall short of or overlap the ends of the slab or a control joint by less than 1 inch, adjust the spacing between the tiles so they line up. If the misalignment exceeds 1 inch, lay the dry run from the middle of the slab. Mark for cutting any tiles that overlap edges or control joints.

ESTIMATING MATERIALS

Pavers and quarries are sold by the carton, each holding enough for 15 square feet. Figure the square footage of the slab and add 5 percent for waste. The thin-set mortar for affixing the tiles comes in 20- to 50-pound bags; 10 pounds covers 15 square feet. Grout—used to fill the joints between tiles—comes in 5- and 10-pound bags and is available in colors; one pound will cover 1 square foot Measure the lengths of control joints in the slab and buy enough foam backer rod for filling expansion joints *(page 171)*.

TOOLS		MATERIALS
■ Rub brick	■ Hacksaw frame with rod saw	■ Latex-modified thin-set mortar
■ Pointing trowel		■ Latex-modified grout
■ Quarry-tile trowel	■ Abrasive stone	■ Foam backer rod
■ Broom	■ Utility knife	■ Self-leveling caulk
■ Hammer	■ Rubber grout float	
■ Tile cutter	■ Caulking gun	

SAFETY TIP

Mortar and grout are caustic—wear gloves when working with them; add goggles and a dust mask when mixing them. Always protect your eyes with goggles when cutting tile. Put on a dust mask when smoothing a concrete slab.

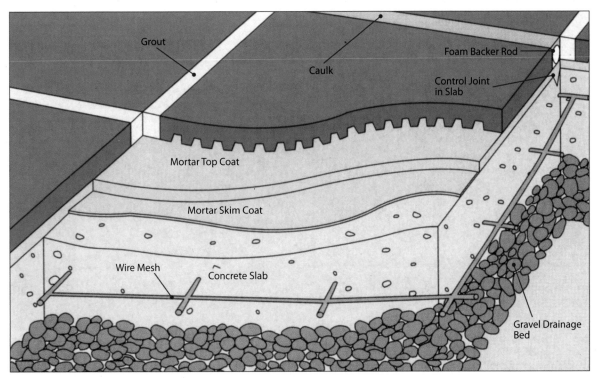

Grout

Caulk

Foam Backer Rod

Control Joint
in Slab

Mortar Top Coat

Mortar Skim Coat

Wire Mesh

Concrete Slab

Gravel Drainage
Bed

Anatomy of tile paving

Tiles are laid over a flat concrete slab reinforced with wire mesh. The slab rests on a gravel drainage bed and is sloped so water will flow off. A bed of thin-set mortar—Portland cement modified with a latex additive—comprises two layers: a skim coat that bonds the mortar to the slab, and a thicker top coat that anchors the tiles. Joints between the tiles are packed with grout; while those that line up over control joints in the slab are filled with foam backer rod and caulk, enabling tiles to move without cracking.

Applying the skim coat

Dampen the slab with a wet broom. With the flat edge of the quarry-tile trowel, scoop one-half a trowelful of mortar onto the underside of the blade. Starting at one end of the slab and holding the flat edge of the trowel against the surface at a 45-degree angle, press the tool down firmly and spread a paper-thin coating of mortar about 3 feet long *(right)*.

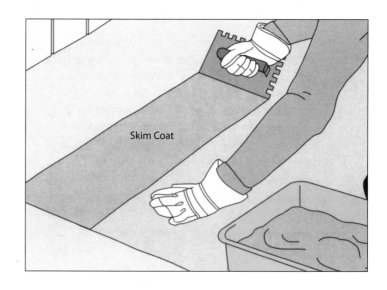

Skim Coat

Applying the top coat

Before the skim coat hardens, scoop more mortar—this time a trowelful—onto the underside of the trowel, and spread a layer of mortar ¼ inch thick over the skim coat. Once the skim coat is covered, press the notched edge of the trowel against the surface at a 45-degree angle and comb the mortar, forming a series of ridges *(left)*.

LAYING THE TILE

Seating the first tile
Position the first tile at the corner of the slab, aligning its outside edges with those of the slab. Press the tile down into the mortar bed, pushing it across the lines of mortar a little then back into position to coat its underside *(left)*.

Spacing tiles
Lay a second tile next to the first, separating them with a ³/₈-inch spacer *(right)*, or by the width obtained during your dry run *(page 170)*. Tiles with lugs are self-spacing, but you may need to adjust them as well to match their dry-run positions. Plastic tile spacers *(photograph)* can also be fitted against the corners of tiles as they are laid; these are left in place until the mortar cures. Align the edges of the two tiles.

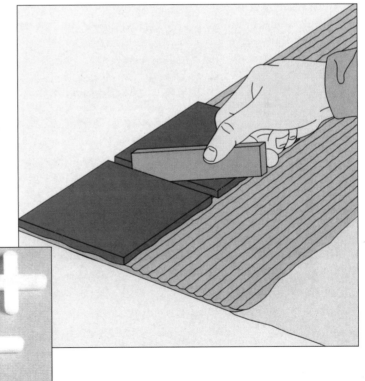

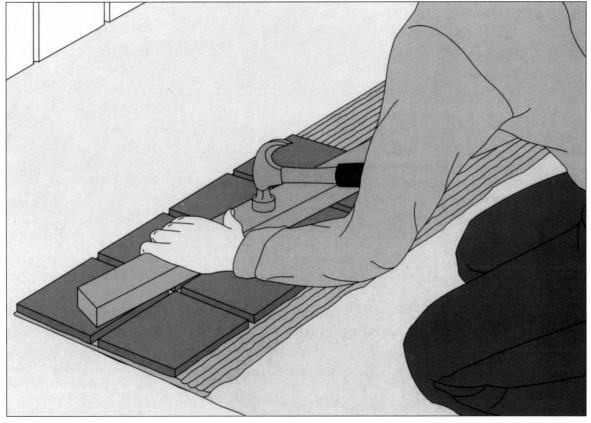

Truing the tile bed

After laying six or eight tiles, check that they lie flat and even by setting a long, straight board diagonally across them—there should be no gaps between the tiles and the board. To flatten the bed, tap the board gently with a hammer *(above)*. Place the board along the outside edges of the tiles and tap any crooked ones into alignment. Sponge any excess mortar from the tiles. Repeat the process across the slab, aligning joints between tiles directly over control joints in the slab. You can stop work at any point, but be sure to clean the tiles before wrapping up. Once you have covered the slab, let the mortar cure for the amount of time specified on the package, then remove any spacers.

FILLING THE JOINTS

Preparing the grout

Into a clean pail, pour the amount of liquid latex additive recommended on the grout bag. Slowly add the grout, mixing with a pointing trowel *(right)*. Keep a record of the amounts of liquid and grout so you can duplicate them in future batches—and avoid any color variations. Continue stirring until the mixture is smooth and evenly colored. Let the grout sit for about 5 minutes, then remix it.

Grouting the joints

With a utility knife, clean mortar from the joints between the tiles. Stuff rolled newspaper into the gaps above control joints in the slab. Pour 1 or 2 cups of the grout mixture onto the tiles. Holding a rubber grout float at a 45-degree angle, drag the grout diagonally across the tiles *(left)*; press down hard enough to pack the grout into the joints and force out air pockets. Work on an area of about 5 square feet at a time. Holding the trowel almost perpendicular to the surface, scrape off excess grout. Wait 15 minutes, then wipe the surface with a damp sponge. Grout the remaining tiles the same way. Once the grout begins to harden and a haze appears on the tiles, wipe the surface clean with a soft cloth.

Rolled
Newspaper

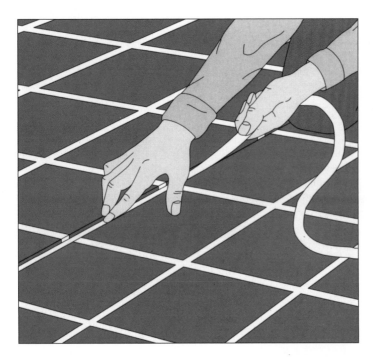

Filling the control joints

Once the grout has cured for the time specified on the bag, remove the newspaper from the control joints. Press foam backer rod slightly larger than the joints into the gaps *(left)*.

Caulking the joints

With a caulking gun, fill the joints with a self-leveling silicone or polyurethane caulk *(right)*. With the solvent recommended by the manufacturer, immediately wipe any caulk from the tiles. Avoid walking on the tiles until the caulk is no longer tacky.

Veneering a House with Brick

Building an outer wall of brick over an inner wood frame is far less costly than constructing a solid brick wall, but yields many of its advantages: Brick is more resistant to weather than wood siding, and it requires very little maintenance.

FOOTING, FOUNDATION, AND EAVES

You can also veneer a house that is already covered with siding—if the building meets certain conditions. The footing must be wide enough to accommodate the extra layer of brickwork. And if the house has a basement, you will need to build a foundation wall of 4-inch concrete blocks to support the bricks. If the footing extends 5 inches beyond the foundation, it is ample for the new wall; otherwise consult a specialist about having the footing extended. You may need to extend the overhang of the eaves as well to accommodate the thicker wall. Submit a plan for the project to the local building department for approval.

PREPARATORY WORK

You will need to cover the existing siding with building paper, extend the window and door casings to be deep enough to meet the new brickwork, and locate wall studs for attaching the wall ties that will anchor the brickwork to the existing walls. One wall tie is set for every 12 bricks, although on gables you will need one for every six bricks.

The final step in planning is to plot the placement of courses, which may have to be adjusted vertically in order to avoid splitting bricks horizontally as you build around windows and doors and under the soffit at the eaves *(page 182)*. If you plan to enliven the brickwork with quoins, decorative patterns, or arches, draw a section of the wall on graph paper.

Rent scaffolding, and plan to do your bricklaying in good weather, when neither rain nor freezing temperatures will adversely affect the mortar.

TOOLS
- Level
- Hammer
- Mason's line
- Mason's trowel
- Jointing tool
- Jointer

MATERIALS
- 2 x 4s
- Common nails (3½")
- Galvanized common nails (2½")
- Roofing nails (1")
- Bricks
- Mortar
- Polyethylene sheeting (6-mil)
- Steel wall ties
- Rope or ⅜-inch tubing
- Steel lintels (¼" × 3½" × 3½")
- Molding

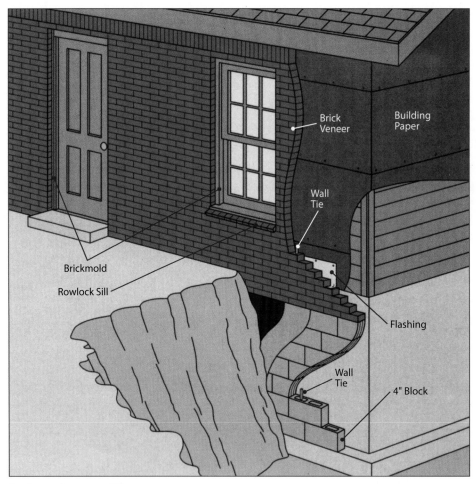

Brick Veneer

Building Paper

Wall Tie

Brickmold

Rowlock Sill

Flashing

Wall Tie

4" Block

Anatomy of a veneered house

The brick facing added to a wood-frame house rests on a 4-inch-wide concrete-block foundation built on the outer ledge of the house footing, but separated from the foundation by a 1-inch air space. At every two courses of block and at 6-foot intervals, corrugated-steel wall ties are anchored in the mortar joints and nailed to the existing foundation with 2½-inch masonry nails. The block foundation rises to a point that will allow the first three courses of brick to be laid below grade, and is damp-proofed. Overlapping sheets of building paper protect the siding from moisture. The veneer bricks stand 1 inch away from the siding; wall ties anchor them every six courses to the wall studs. Steel lintels provide support over windows and doors. Moisture is directed out of the air space with flashing and rope wicks placed at the bottom of the veneer wall, above windows and doors, and below sills. Brickmold—wood molding 1 inch thick and 2½ inches wide—is added to window and door frames. Below each existing window sill, rowlocks—bricks set on edge—create a second sill, angled to shed water.

ALIGNING COURSES

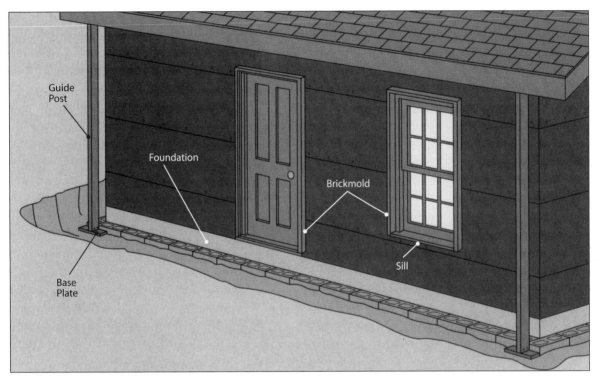

Guide Post

Foundation

Brickmold

Sill

Base Plate

A system for marking course levels

To keep from having to split bricks horizontally to fit at doors, windows, or the soffit, mark course heights in advance. Set two straight 2-by-4s, one at each end of the wall, on wood base plates so the distance between their inner faces and the wall is equal to the thickness of a brick, plus 1 inch for the air space between the wall and veneer. Plumb the posts and toenail them to the plates and the soffit, and mark on them a whole number of courses between the foundation and the bottom of the rowlock sills,

which will extend 4½ inches below the existing window sills. If sills are at different heights, choose one as a reference—the one at which split bricks would be most conspicuous. To arrive at whole-brick courses, you can vary the width of mortar joints from ¼ inch to ½ inch. In the same way, measure and mark the courses between the bottom of the rowlock sills and the top of the wood brickmold on the windows and doors. Measure and mark the courses between the brickmold and the soffit.

RAISING THE VENEER

Laying the first course

As shown in the inset, start at the right and lay a dry row of bricks along the top of the block foundation: Place the first brick 5 inches beyond the corner of the house, and adjust the width of the mortar joints so that the last brick—including the measurement for the mortar joint on the outside end—extends 1 inch beyond the far corner. Stretch a mason's line at the first-course markings on the guide posts. Set aside three or four bricks at a time, spread a bed of mortar on the foundation, then butter the ends of the bricks and position them in the mortar (right).

House Wall

Last Brick   1"   First Brick   5"

A CONVENIENT BRICK TOTE

The task of shifting bricks from storage to work site can be made substantially easier with steel brick tongs (photograph). Place the tongs around the row of bricks you want to lift and raise the handle— the ends clamp tight. When you set the bricks down, the tongs release their hold. Depending on the model, the tool can be adjusted to accommodate different numbers of bricks—from as few as six to as many as eleven.

Flashing the brickwork

Add three courses of bricks in order to bring the top of the brick veneer just above ground level. For each course, align the bricks with the mason's line at the corresponding marks on the guide posts, and to allow for a doorstep do not place any bricks beneath the door opening; cut the bricks that will abut the step. As you work, use the trowel to remove any excess mortar that may have squeezed into the air space behind the bricks. Spread a 12-inch strip of 6-mil polyethylene sheeting along the top course of bricks and up the house wall, adjusting it so that the lower edge lies 1 inch from the outer face of the bricks; fasten the other edge to the wall with closely spaced 1-inch roofing nails *(right)*. Spread a bed of mortar over the plastic and lay the next course of bricks as you did the last, but insert a piece of rope or ³/₈-inch tubing as long as a brick is wide at the base of every second mortar joint in this course *(inset)* to allow moisture to escape from the wall.

Rope

Anchoring the veneer

Moving up the mason's line on the guide posts as you go, lay subsequent courses of bricks with the vertical joints staggered and the ends of the courses forming a stepped diagonal away from the corners of the house. Cut any bricks abutting doors or windows to fit flush with the brickmold. When the veneer is six courses high, bend corrugated wall ties at their midpoint to form a right angle. Rest one leg of the tie on the brickwork and nail the other leg of the angle to a wall stud with 2½-inch galvanized common nails *(left)*. Spread mortar and lay the next course of bricks, embedding the ties firmly in the masonry. For the adjacent wall, set up guide posts, marked as for the front wall, then lay the bricks and anchor them with wall ties in the same way as you did for the front wall. When you have covered about a third of the height of the wall, leaving a 4½-inch gap beneath any windows *(page 182)*, lay the corner sections of courses, wrapping each course around onto the adjacent wall as you work. Lay the adjacent corners of the other walls in this way, completing one-third of the height of each wall at a time and finishing the mortar joints *(page 22)* before moving to the next section.

DEALING WITH WINDOWS AND DOORS

Positioning the lintel

Across the top of each door or window opening, lay a ¼- by 3½- by 3½-inch steel lintel that extends at least 8 inches beyond the opening on either side. Align the vertical flange of the lintel so that its front face is flush with the back face of the bricks on which it rests. Fill in the ½-inch space between the front face of the bricks and the front edge of the lintel with a band of mortar, scraped from the back of the trowel *(right)*.

Vertical Flange of Lintel

Setting bricks over the lintel

Cut a strip of 12-inch-wide 6-mil polyethylene sheeting the length of the lintel, then position and nail it *(page 181)*. Adjust the mason's line and lay the next course of bricks; over the lintel, join the bricks end to end with mortar, omitting the bed of mortar beneath them *(left)*, and inserting lengths of rope or ³/₈-inch tubing at every second joint.

CAPPING THE WALL

Laying the final bricks

When the veneer wall is three courses below the eave, set up the mason's line ¼ inch below the eave, and spread a mortar bed over a section of the last course of horizontal bricks. Butter one bed side of each brick for the final course and stand it on the mortar bed, lining up the top of the brick with the mason's line *(above)*. Continue to lay the vertical bricks, but set the last six bricks dry and equally spaced, then mark their positions on the course below and remove them. Mortar the six bricks in place. For a gable wall, raise the wall to the eave level, then erect three-course leads at both ends of the topmost course *(inset)*, cutting the outer bricks at an angle to fit snugly under the sloping eave. String a mason's line between the leads, anchored into the mortar with nails, then lay the intermediate bricks, anchoring the bricks to the wall with a wall tie every third course; repeat the process until the veneer wall is completed. Cover the ragged edge of the sloping brickwork with a strip of molding or an overhanging frieze board.

A ROWLOCK SILL

Setting the end bricks

Seal the 4 ½-inch opening below each window with a 12-inch-wide strip of 6-mil polyethylene sheeting, nailed to the backup wall *(page 181)*. Cut two bricks to 5 inches in length and mortar them in place at the ends of the opening, angling them slightly downward. Check that both bricks protrude equally from the wall face—usually ½ inch—and hold a level across the tops of the bricks to be sure they lie at the same angle.

Adding intermediate bricks

Cut more 5-inch bricks and set them in place dry to space the joints, marking their positions on the window sill. Adjust the mason's line until it runs level with the tops of the end bricks, holding it flush by folding scraps of cardboard around the line at the end bricks and clamping them down under scrap bricks placed on top of the end bricks. Butter and lay the sill bricks, aligning them with the marks and the line *(above)*, and inserting pieces of rope or ³/₈-inch tubing at every second mortar joint. Finish the mortar joints.

A BLOCK WALL FACED WITH BRICK

When brick veneer is backed by a concrete-block wall, the bricks and blocks rise together, with a 1-inch air space between them; the local building code will dictate the total required thickness of the wall. Both the concrete-block backup wall—here 4 inches thick—and the brick veneer share a concrete footing (pages 92–94). The two layers are tied together at every sixth brick course with joint-reinforcement wire straddling both layers. Because no existing wall is present to support guide posts for the courses, stepped-back corner leads are erected for both layers. Steel joint-reinforcement wire is installed in the leads, cut 12 inches longer than the lead so that it will overlap the reinforcement wire in the intermediate blocks to be laid later. Flashing is also installed in the appropriate courses of the corner leads, and is cut 4 inches longer than the lead to overlap the flashing on the bricks between the leads. The flashing is placed in the same locations as for brick veneer over wood siding, and is anchored to mortar joints in the backup wall.

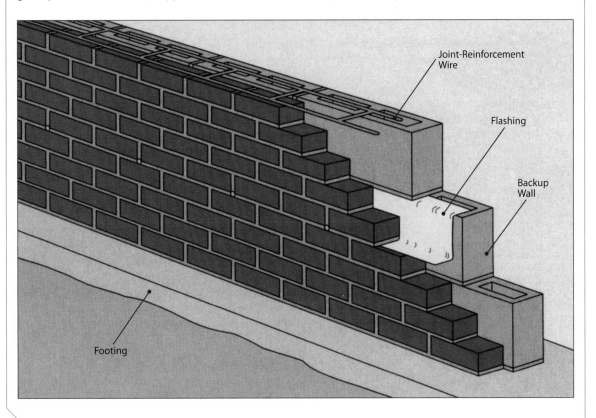

Joint-Reinforcement Wire

Flashing

Backup Wall

Footing

Paving with Stone

No masonry material is more handsome or durable than flagstone, the rough-cut stone most commonly used for paving. Also known as flagging, it is available in several types *(opposite)*.

PAVING METHODS

Flagstones can be laid in sand, but the stones may shift and need to be reseated occasionally. For a more maintenance-free paving, lay the stones over a concrete slab, anchoring them in mortar and grouting the joints. Cement butter, a mixture of cement and water, is spread under each stone to strengthen its bond to the mortar. Tiles made of stone, such as marble or slate, are laid the same way as ceramic tiles *(page 170)*.

PREPARING FOR THE JOB

Flagstone is sold by the square foot. Buy enough for the area to be covered, adding about 10 percent for waste. For the mortar, grout, and cement butter, estimate 150 pounds of Portland cement and 500 pounds of concrete sand—a coarser variety for mixing concrete—for every 50 square feet of paving.

Before delivery day, clear a space close to the work site and spread out tarpaulins or plastic sheeting on the lawn.

WORKING WITH STONE

Flagstones are awkward to lift—for a solid grip, wedge them up with a prybar. For moving stones, consider renting a dolly.

TOOLS		MATERIALS
■ Maul	■ Mason's level	■ Stakes
■ Shovel	■ Stiff-bristled broom	■ String
■ 2 x 4 screed	■ Soft-bristled brush	■ Concrete sand
■ Tamper	■ Mason's Towel	■ Wood strips
■ Stonemason's hammer	■ Pointing trowel	■ Portland cement
■ Stone chisel	■ Concave jointer	
■ Rubber mallet		

SAFETY TIP

Wear goggles when trimming or splitting stone; you may also want to don gloves to protect your hands from the rough edges. Put on hard-toed shoes when handling stone. Mortar is caustic—wear gloves when working with it, and goggles and a dust mask when mixing it. Use goggles, a dust mask, and long sleeves and pants when working with a grinder.

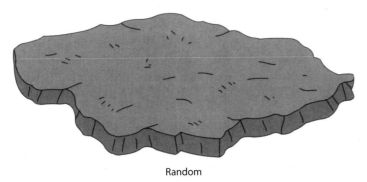

Random

Rectangular

Types of flagstone

Flagging is made by splitting stone such as slate, bluestone, limestone, and sandstone into thin slabs. Your choice will be limited by the types of stone available in your area. Flagstones are commonly available in random shapes or cut roughly into rectangles as shown at left. They can also be purchased trimmed to precise patterns. Stones range in size from ½ to 4 square feet in area and from ½ to 2½ inches thick. For a sand bed, flags should be 1½ to 2 inches thick; for a mortar bed, ½ to 1 inch thick.

LAYING FLAGSTONES IN SAND

Fitting stones

Stake the area you plan to cover *(page 82)*, excavate it to a depth of 3 inches, and lay down a 2-inch layer of concrete sand, following the technique on page 86. Starting at one corner, arrange six or seven flagstones on the sand bed. Line up straight edges with the edges of the bed and fit irregular edges together so joints will be about ½ inch wide. With a pencil, mark overlapping segments to be trimmed *(right)*.

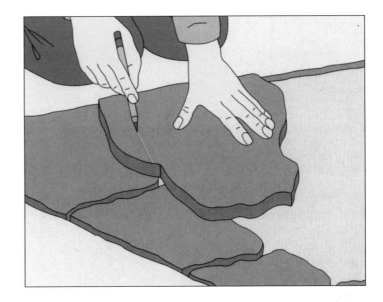

AN ALUMINUM-FOIL TEMPLATE

To accurately mark stones for trimming, make an aluminum-foil template. Set a piece of aluminum foil in the space to be filled and cut or fold it to fit, allowing for ½-inch joints. Set the template on a stone of approximately the right size and shape, and trace around the pattern with a pencil to mark the cutting lines.

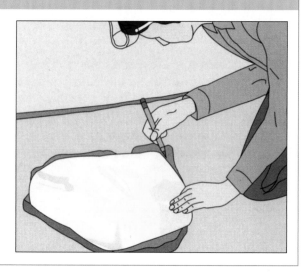

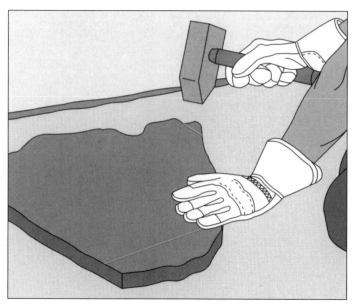

Trimming small segments

Place the stone on the sand bed. Chip off small pieces by striking them outside the pencil marks with a stonemason's hammer or a bricklayer's hammer (left). Save the chips to serve as fillers between stones. When a segment is hard to remove, undercut by chipping away bits from the bottom edge; then, try trimming it again.

A RIGHT-ANGLE GRINDER FOR EASY CUTS

If cutting stone by hand seems arduous, consider renting a right-angle grinder. Designed for grinding and polishing stone, the tool can also be fitted with a diamond blade for cutting. Wear the safety gear recommended on page 186, and practice on scrap stone until you are comfortable with the technique. Turn on the grinder with the blade clear of the stone and, holding the tool upright, score the cutting line with a light pass; then apply gentle pressure to make the cut.

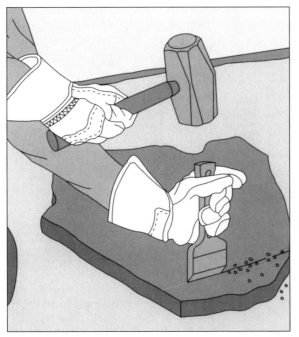

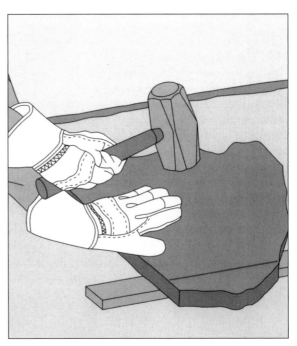

Splitting off large segments

Place the stone on the sand bed and score the drawn line with a maul and a stone chisel *(above, left)*; or, use a brick set in place of a chisel. Prop the stone on a board with the waste segment tilted up beyond the edge of the board. With the maul, tap the segment *(above, right)* until it falls off. If the stone does not split readily, score it along the sides and back, then prop it up and tap it again.

Embedding the stones

With a rubber mallet, tap each stone down into the sand bed so its top lies about ½ inch above ground *(right)*.

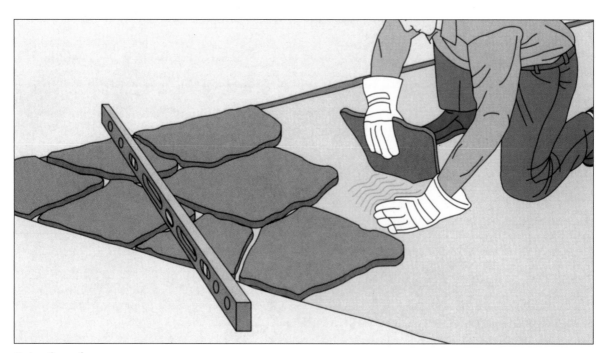

Truing the surface

Set a mason's level across the stones to check if they are even. Brush additional sand under low stones and scoop sand out from under high ones *(above)*. Repeat these steps until you have covered the entire bed with stones.

Filling the joints

Shovel more sand over the flagging and, with a stiff-bristled broom, sweep it across the stones to fill the joints to the top. Wet the surface with a fine water spray and let it dry. Repeat the joint-filling and spraying process until the joints are flush with the stones.

SETTING FLAGS IN A BED OF MORTAR

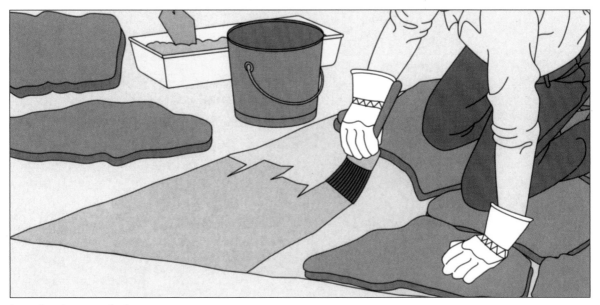

Preparing the mortar bed

If you do not have an existing concrete slab, cast one as described on pages 82 to 86. Arrange stones on the slab in a dry run, leaving no more than 3/4 inch between them. Trim the stones as necessary (pages 188–189). In one container, prepare a batch of mortar from one part Portland cement, four parts masonry sand, and just enough water so the mortar holds the shape of a ball when you grasp it. In a separate container, make cement butter: Portland cement blended with enough water to give it the consistency of soft butter. Remove three or four stones from the slab and wet the concrete with a soft-bristled brush (above).

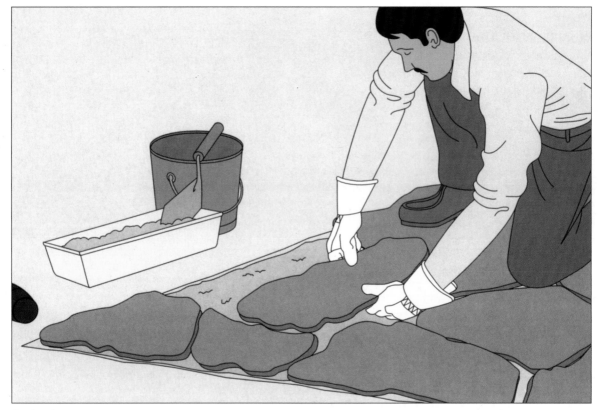

Setting the stones

With a mason's trowel, spread the mortar 1 inch thick over the dampened section of the slab. Reposition the stones *(above)* and, with a rubber mallet, tap them down about ½ inch into the mortar. When you have set about a dozen stones in the mortar, level them *(page 190)*.

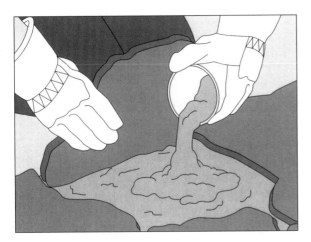

Applying cement butter

Immediately after leveling the stones, pick up one flagstone at a time from the mortar bed and, with a small container, dribble about ¼ cup of cement butter evenly over the bed *(left)*. Replace the stone and tap it back into position with the mallet. When you have buttered all the stones, recheck the level.

Raking the joints

With the tip of a pointing trowel, pack the mortar between the stones under their edges *(right)*. Scrape out excess mortar so the bottoms of the joints are about at the level of the bottoms of the stones. Sponge mortar off the flagging. Let the mortar cure for 24 hours.

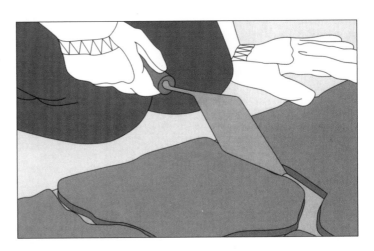

Mortaring the joints

Prepare a batch of mortar *(page 17)*. With the tip of a concave jointer, push mortar into the joints between the flagstones and compact it *(left)*. Sponge off the excess; let the mortar dry for 24 hours before walking on the paving.

Constructing Walls of Natural Stone

Few masonry materials are more attractive or enduring than stone. Natural or quarried rubble produces the most rustic-looking walls, but requires trial and error to arrange. Square-cut stones that create gridded wall patterns need less experimentation as you go along. A simple dry wall *(pages 195–199)*—requiring neither mortar nor footing—may need occasional maintenance if stones become dislodged; a wet wall *(pages 199–200)*—laid over a footing and mortared—is relatively maintenance-free. If you plan on building a wall higher than 3 feet, check local building codes for restrictions.

A NEW ENGLAND DRY WALL

Built directly on the ground or on a bed of gravel, a dry stone wall has overlapping joints like a running-bond brick wall. The wall slopes in two directions—the base is wider and longer than the top—and stones tilt downward toward the center so the gravitational pull compacts the wall and keeps it intact. You can use stones picked up from fields, but they may require considerable cutting to make them join securely. Most builders buy quarried rubble; easily workable types—bluestone, sandstone, or limestone—are best. Don't be too meticulous; a rough wall generally looks better and is sturdier than a fussily even one.

A MORTARED WET WALL

This style of construction is often used for retaining walls, and requires weep holes and gravel fill to drain off water. Like a dry wall, it is tapered inward to keep the stones in place. Stones that are roughly rectangular are easier to build with than rubble; mortar them together over a 6-inch-thick concrete base 18 inches wide or less.

ESTIMATING MATERIALS

Stone for walls is sold either by volume or weight. To calculate your needs in cubic yards, multiply the length, width, and height of the wall in feet, divide the result by 27, and add 10 percent for waste. For the amount of stone needed in pounds, multiply the volume in cubic feet by 125. For a rough estimate of mortar needed, divide the volume of the wall by 5.

TOOLS
- Shovel
- Tamper
- 1 x 2s for slope gauge
- Level
- Stonemason's hammer
- Mason's trowel

MATERIALS
- Gravel
- Plastic tubing (1")
- Mortar ingredients (Portland cement, masonry sand, hydrated lime)

SAFETY TIP

Wear gloves and hard-toed shoes when handling stones. Put on gloves to work with mortar, and goggles and a dust mask when mixing it.

A DRY STONE WALL

A SLOPE GAUGE FOR TAPERED WALLS

To help you lay the stones of a dry wall for an inward taper, make a slope gauge from two 1-by-2s as long as the wall height—3 feet in this case. Fasten these arms together at one end with a single nail and pivot them so the distance between their outside edges at the free end equals 1 inch for each foot of wall height. Secure the free ends with a short two-piece wood block as shown at right. Finally, drive a second nail to lock the pivoting ends together.

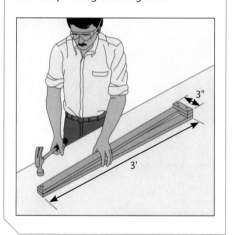

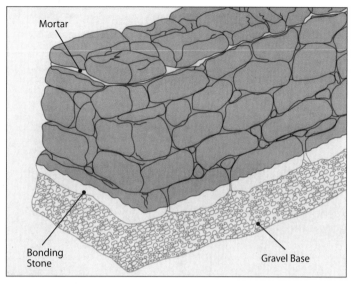

Anatomy of a dry wall

The wall sits in a 6-inch trench on a 5-inch layer of gravel. At one end of the base is a bonding stone that spans the width of the wall. Square-cut stones are laid flat, whereas rubble pieces tilt toward the center of the wall. The base is 2 to 3 feet wide, but each new course is slightly inset to taper the wall inward. Vertical joints in successive courses are staggered. The top layer of stones is often anchored in mortar to seal out water.

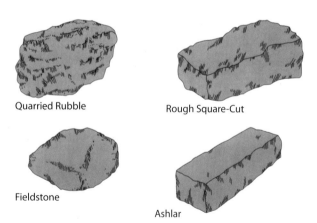

Quarried Rubble

Rough Square-Cut

Fieldstone

Ashlar

Rubble vs. square-cut stone

Rubble is uncut stone, either quarried or obtained as natural field and river stones. The rough surface of quarried rubble holds mortar better than the worn surfaces of field or river stones. Most dealers sell only quarried rubble, in pieces 6 to 18 inches in diameter. Square-cut stone is roughly trimmed. A more precisely shaped—and expensive—version is called ashlar. Widths generally range from 3 to 5 inches, heights from 2 to 8 inches, and lengths from 1 to 4 feet.

BUILDING WITH MORTARLESS STONE

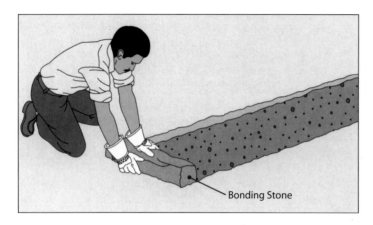

Bonding Stone

Setting the bonding stone
Dig a 6-inch trench to the length and width of the wall. Fill the trench with about 5 inches of gravel and tamp it down. Pick an even-faced stone as long as the wall width and set it at one end as a bonding stone *(left)*. If no stone is long enough to span the trench, lay two stones.

Laying the first course
Use the largest stones for the first course; reserve the flattest ones for the top. Lay four or five stones along one side of the wall, setting them flat rather than on end or on their sides. Orient long pieces lengthwise along the edge of the trench, not across it *(right)*. Place the stones so any slope on the upper surface angles downward to the center of the wall. Alternate between large and small stones, thick and thin ones. Repeat along the other side of the trench.

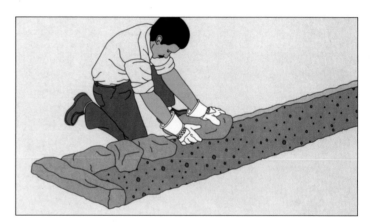

Filling in the middle
Fill in the center of the trench with small stones *(left)*, building up the middle section level with the edges. Continue laying stones along the sides and middle of the trench until you reach the opposite end.

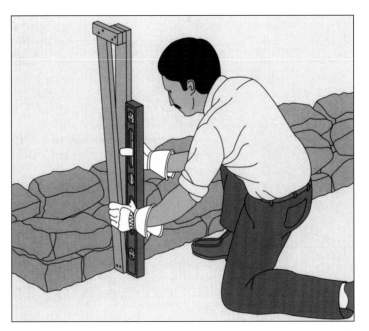

Laying the second course

Choose a stone long enough to overlap the bonding stone and the piece next to it in the first course. Place the stone along one edge of the wall so its top surface angles down slightly toward the center of the wall and its outside edge is set in a little from the underlying stone. Alternating from one side of the wall to the other, continue laying second-course stones that overlap joints in the first course, fit well with the stones underneath, and allow the top of the course to remain level. To check the inward taper of each stone, hold your slope gauge against the wall, and plumb it with a level *(left)*. If the stones do not align with the gauge, reposition them as necessary. Fill in the center of the course.

Shimming

Lay the third course of stones in the same way as the second. Where a stone can be teetered from side to side, insert stone chips or small rocks as shims under an edge *(above)*, pushing them in so they are hidden. Ensure that the stone rests securely and tilts inward.

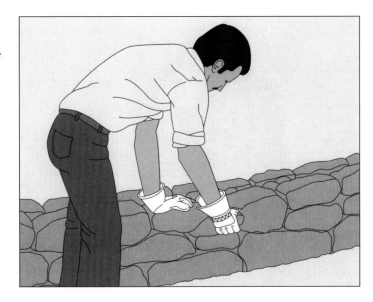

Chinking

Every three courses, fill in fist-sized or larger spaces in the wall by driving narrow stones into the gaps with a stonemason's hammer *(right)*. Leave smaller gaps alone. Keep each course level and check the taper of the wall with the slope gauge.

Mortaring the final course

Once you've laid the next-to-last course, prepare a batch of mortar *(pages 17–18)*. With a mason's trowel, cover the top course of stones with a 1-inch layer of mortar. Set the flat stones you reserved into the mortar *(left)*. Fill in the gaps between these stones with mortar, sloping the joints down from the middle out to the edges to prevent water from pooling on the wall. Trim excess mortar from the sides of the wall with the trowel. Once the mortar is thumbprint-hard, use a small piece of wood to rake the joints along the sides of the wall to a depth of about 1 inch.

DEALING WITH A CORNER

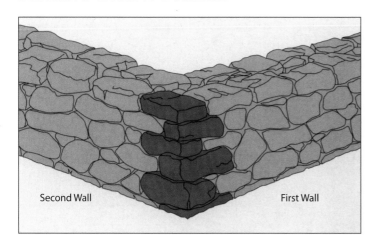

Second Wall   First Wall

Interlocking the stones
Build up the first and second walls course by course as you would for a straight wall, but at the corner, use large stones (shaded area in walls at right) to make the 90-degree turn from the first wall to the second wall.

A MORTARED RETAINING WALL

A stone retaining wall
The low, 18-inch-wide wall at right sits on a concrete footing 12 inches thick. The wall is built with square-cut stones laid out with ¾-inch-wide mortar joints and stacked so vertical joints are staggered as much as possible. Weep holes every 3 to 4 feet at the bottom lead water away from the soil behind the wall, and gravel banked in the trench behind the wall will enable water to seep down to the weep holes. If the soil is very fine, the fill can be kept clean by covering it with a layer of filter fabric, available at landscaping suppliers.

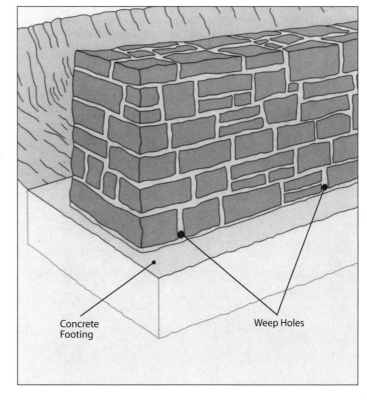

Concrete
Footing   Weep Holes

PROPS IN A RUBBLE WALL

If you're building a mortared wall with rubble, the weight of large, irregular stones can squeeze mortar from joints. To support the stones, push small wood shims *(right)* under larger stones as you lay them. Once the mortar is hard, pull out the shims and fill the gaps with mortar.

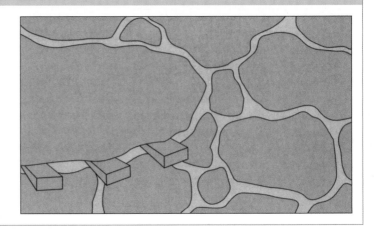

Raking the joints

On the top of the wall, lay and mortar a course of flat stones as for a dry wall *(page 198)*. Rake the joints between stones with a small piece of scrap wood *(above)*, compacting the mortar and removing it to a depth of about 1 inch. After the mortar has set for a day or so, fill in behind the wall with gravel to within 6 inches of the top of the wall. Then cover the gravel with topsoil.

Concrete Block for Economical Construction

Concrete block gives the builder two major advantages over other types of masonry: economy and speed. A block wall costs less per running foot than a brick wall of an equivalent size, and takes about half as long to build. The gain over stone is many times greater.

PREPARING TO BUILD A WALL

Like a brick wall, a block wall is set on a concrete footing (*pages 92–94*). Low walls—up to 3 feet high—are easiest to build. Taller walls are likely to require reinforcement (*page 160*), although in some areas even low walls require reinforcement. Check your local codes before beginning the job.

The mortar for block walls is stiffer than that for bricks. Reduce the water in the mortar recipe (*pages 17–18*) so that the mixture will not simply slip from a trowel but must be shaken off.

BUILDING WITH BLOCKS

Blocks come in a variety of shapes and sizes, each with a different function or design (*page 202*). For optimal wall strength, lay them in the running-bond pattern (*page 161*).

Blocks can be cut in the same way as bricks (*page 28*); or you can use a circular saw fitted with a masonry blade or rent a masonry saw.

To seal the top of the wall from water, lay solid-top blocks for the last course, or fill the cores of the top-course blocks with mortar and add a coping of brick or ½-inch flagstone (*page 206*).

TOOLS
- Mason's trowel
- Mason's line and blocks
- Mason's level
- Tin snips
- Convex jointer
- Shovel

MATERIALS
- Mortar ingredients: Portland cement, hydrated lime, masonry sand
- Metal mesh
- Thin-set mortar
- Small flagstones

SAFETY TIP

Mortar is caustic—wear gloves when working with it, and goggles and a dust mask when mixing it. Also don gloves when handling concrete blocks to protect your hands from the rough edges. Put on hard-toed shoes to prevent injury from dropped or falling blocks.

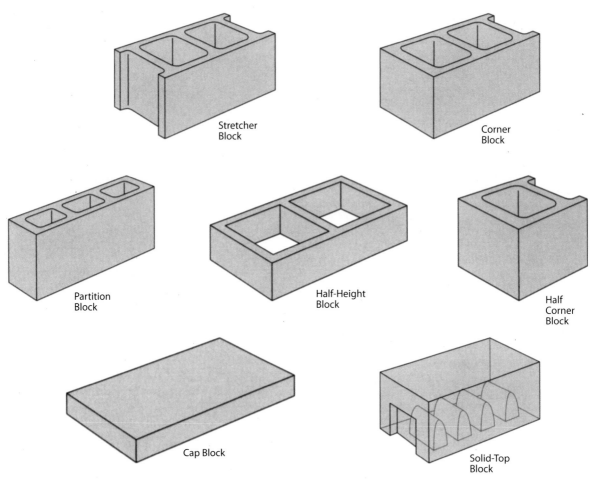

Stretcher Block

Corner Block

Partition Block

Half-Height Block

Half Corner Block

Cap Block

Solid-Top Block

A block for every purpose

Blocks of lighter-weight concrete are available, but a standard stretcher block weighs about 30 pounds and measures 8 by 8 by 16 inches. It has mortar-joint projections at both ends and two hollow cores bordered by partitions called webs. A variation of the stretcher, the corner block, is flat on one end for use at corners. Half-corner blocks laid at the end of every second course enable vertical joints to be staggered in a running-bond pattern;

you can buy half blocks or cut them yourself from corner units. Partition and half-height blocks can be used as cores in brick structures. Partition blocks can also provide weep holes in retaining walls *(page 199)*. Solid-top or cap units are handy for capping block walls. Special "architectural" blocks with different surface textures are also available, as well as screen blocks for decorative effect.

MORTARLESS BLOCKS

A variation on the standard concrete block is a type that does not need mortar. The unit at right, for example, has pins that slip into predrilled holes and lock the block to one above it. The block is tapered from front to back at each end, making it possible to build curved walls. In a straight wall, every other block is reversed.

ERECTING A BLOCK WALL

Projection   Web   Face Shell

Laying the blocks

If local codes dictate that the wall must be reinforced *(page 160)*, add steel reinforcements according to code specifications. For a wall that needs no reinforcement, first throw and furrow a bed of mortar 1½ inches thick on the footing *(pages 18–19)*. Build stepped leads at the ends of the wall, adapting the technique for a brick wall *(pages 161–163)*, starting with a corner block at each end. For convenience, butter two blocks at a time: Stand them on end on the ground and spread mortar on their projections. Then, lay each block, lifting it by its outside webs and pushing it into the mortar bed and against the adjacent block, forming a ³⁄₈-inch mortar joint. Trowel away any extruded mortar. For subsequent courses, throw a mortar line two blocks long along the face shells of the previous course. Start and end every second course with a half corner block so vertical joints can be staggered. Periodically check for alignment and level as you lay the blocks. Once the leads are completed, fill in between them *(page 164)*, using a mason's line to keep the wall straight. For a wall longer than 20 feet, add control joints *(page 207)*. Rainproof the wall *(page 205)* one course from the top. When the mortar is thumbprint hard, finish the joints with a convex jointer *(page 22)*.

RAINPROOFING THE TOP

Core

Mesh

Filling the cores

Before throwing the mortar for the final course of blocks, use tin snips to cut metal mesh or hardware cloth into strips two blocks long and 1 inch wider than the cores. Apply the mortar for the top course and push the mesh into it. Lay the blocks on the mortar and mesh *(above)*. Trowel mortar into the cores, filling them even with the tops of the webs.

A HANDY FUNNEL FOR FILLING BLOCKS

To speed up the process of filling the last course of blocks with mortar, build a funnel from ½-inch plywood. Cut the sides to the distance between the outside webs of a stretcher block and the ends Y-shaped to fit into the cores. To fill the blocks, use mortar thinned down just enough to be pourable.

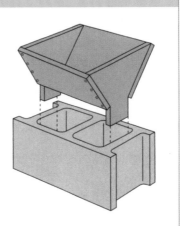

Adding a coping

For increased weather protection, use thin-set mortar as for tile *(page 170)*. Trowel a ½-inch mortar bed on top of the last course of blocks. In areas subject to freezing temperatures, spread the mortar higher along one edge of the wall than the other so the coping will slope and prevent water from pooling on the wall. Set small flagstones on the mortar, leaving ⅜ inch of space between the pieces *(right)*. Fill the joints with mortar *(page 175)*.

DEALING WITH SPECIAL SITUATIONS

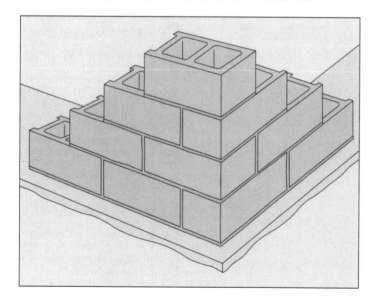

Corner leads

For a wall with corners, first build corner leads as shown at left. The leads should step up half a block with each course, and the blocks at the corner should overlap. Once the leads are erected, fill in between them with blocks.

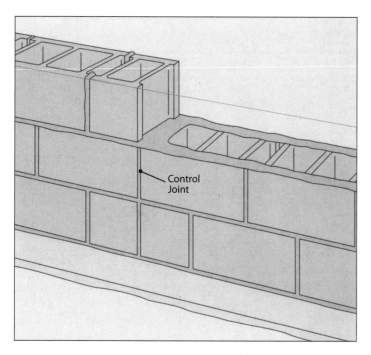

Control joints for long walls

Block walls more than 20 feet long may develop cracks over time. Such cracking can be confined to weaker control joints located every 20 feet along the wall. To form the joints, use two half blocks in every other course, creating a continuous vertical joint *(left)*. Once the mortar stiffens, further weaken these joints by raking them to a depth of ¾ inch; fill the recess with caulk.

Control Joint

A BLOCK RETAINING WALL

Anatomy of an earth dam

To hold back the weight of soil, a block retaining wall must be buttressed by pilasters and provided with weep holes for drainage. In the wall at right, block pilasters are erected at each end of a concrete footing and at 10-foot intervals in between. One block shorter in height than the rest of the wall, the pilasters will be covered by the backfill. For drainage, gravel is banked against the back of the wall to allow water to seep down to the weep holes; then it is covered with 6 inches of topsoil. To keep the gravel clean in very fine soil, cover it with a layer of filter fabric (available at a landscaping supplier). Solid-top blocks complete the uppermost course of blocks, or standard blocks can be used, filled with mortar and decorated with a stone coping *(page 206)*.

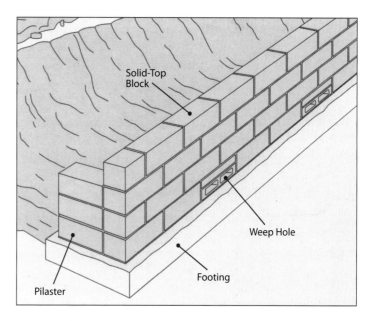

Solid-Top Block

Weep Hole

Footing

Pilaster

RAISING THE STRUCTURE

Preparing the site

Dig a trench about 2 feet wide, clearing 3½-foot niches at the ends and every 10 feet in between for the pilasters. Pile the soil above the excavation so it will be easy to fill in later. Cast a footing for the wall *(pages 92–94)* with a 16-inch-square wing in the niches for each pilaster, as shown at right. Include reinforcing bars if necessary *(opposite)*.

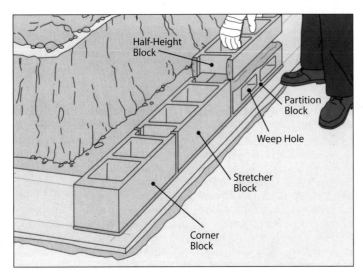

Starting the lead

Starting at one end of the footing, throw a mortar line for three blocks, then lay a corner block and a stretcher, followed by a partition block set on its side so the cores can serve as weep holes. To maintain the first course at a uniform height, spread mortar on the partition block, then butter one end of a half-height block and lay it on top *(left)*. Start another lead the same way at the other end of the footing.

Pilaster

Tying in pilasters

Lay a stretcher block at a right angle to the first block of each lead to form pilasters. Lay the second course of the leads and pilasters, then throw mortar beds for the third course of the leads and pilasters. Cut two pieces of metal mesh or hardware cloth 7 inches wide and about 16 inches long and push each one into the mortar on the pilaster and the first lead block, ½ inch from the front of the wall *(left)*. Fill in between the leads, creating weep holes every third block in the first course and tying a pilaster into the wall at each projection in the footing. If weep holes coincide with a pilaster, offset the holes by one block.

REINFORCING BLOCK WALLS

Depending on local codes, concrete-block walls more than a certain height need reinforcing. In areas with seismic activity, reinforcement is usually required for low walls as well. Requirements are generally even stricter for retaining walls. The size and placement of reinforcing bars (rebars) are also specified by code. For vertical buttressing, rebars are inserted down through the cores and tied with wire to rods cast into the footing. The cores are then filled with grout. For horizontal reinforcement, special webless bond-beam blocks are used. Rebars are set in these blocks, which are then filled with grout. Where rebars are spliced, the pieces should overlap by about 18 inches and be tied together with wire.

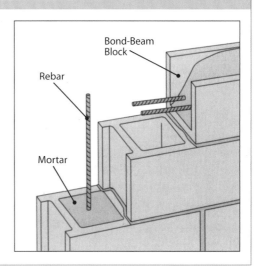

Bond-Beam Block

Rebar

Mortar

A Brick and Block Barbecue

Inexpensive concrete blocks can be covered with bricks to make a permanent freestanding barbecue. The construction job itself falls into two distinct stages: pouring a reinforced concrete slab *(pages 84–86)*, and laying the bricks and blocks.

CHOOSING THE SITE

First consult your local building inspector and fire department to see how codes or permit requirements will affect your plans. Locate the barbecue downwind from your home and neighboring houses, and from the dining area. Orient the structure so the prevailing winds will blow smoke away from the cook and create a draft for the fire.

DESIGNING THE BARBECUE

The barbecue opposite rests on a concrete slab 8 inches thick and large enough to provide a 6-inch skirt around the back and sides and a 2-foot apron in front. You can tailor the design of the barbecue to suit your needs and tastes. Change the height of the grill, for example, by altering the number of brick courses and the height of the block core. You can adapt the shape to accommodate a larger, smaller, or second grill; or increase or decrease counter space: Lay out the first brick courses in the desired pattern and plan the core to fill the interior. It's also possible to add a door, converting the area below the ashpan into a warming oven or a storage area.

ACCESSORIES

The grill, fire grate, and ashpan are all available from masonry supply dealers, hardware stores, or restaurant equipment houses. The grill, made of cast iron or steel, should be rigid and heavy enough to resist sagging and being pushed out of position accidentally. The fire grate is usually made in small sections of heavy cast iron; you will probably need more than one section. Instead of separate grills and grates, you can buy a ready-to-install grate-and-grill system that enables you to adjust the cooking temperature by cranking the grill or grate up and down. The ashpan can be anything from a specially built sheet-metal container to a disposable aluminum broiler pan.

   The stone countertop can be ordered cut to size from a mason supplier after the barbecue is constructed.

TOOLS	MATERIALS
▪ Tape measure	▪ Bricks
▪ Chalk line	▪ Concrete blocks
▪ Carpenter's square	▪ Mortar ingredients (Portland cement, masonry sand, hydrated lime)
▪ Mason's trowel	
▪ Mason's level	
▪ Mason's line	▪ Lumber for story pole
▪ Hacksaw	▪ Wall ties
▪ Joint filler	▪ Rebar (⅜")
▪ Convex jointer	▪ Stone countertop
▪ Straightedge	▪ Resin-based stone sealing compound
▪ Utility knife	
▪ Paintbrush	▪ Grill
	▪ Fire grate
	▪ Ashpan

SAFETY TIP

Mortar is caustic—wear gloves when working with it, and goggles and a dust mask when mixing it. Put on hard-toed shoes when handling bricks or concrete blocks.

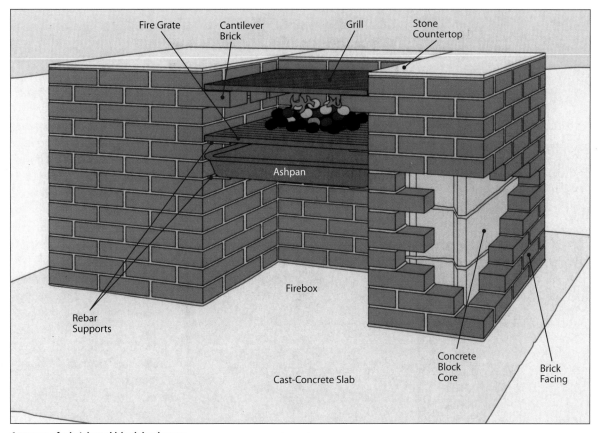

Fire Grate   Cantilever Brick   Grill   Stone Countertop

Ashpan

Rebar Supports

Firebox

Concrete Block Core

Brick Facing

Cast-Concrete Slab

Antomy of a brick and block barbecue

The double-pedestal barbecue above measures about 5½ feet wide by 2½ feet deep and sits on a slab 6½ feet wide and 5 feet deep. Twelve brick courses in a running bond pattern with ½-inch mortar joints will position the grill at about the same height as burners on a kitchen stove. The grill is held by cantilever bricks that project from each pedestal. The fire grate is positioned three brick courses below the grill, and the ashpan another two courses lower. Both the grate and ashpan are supported by stubs of rebar fixed in mortar joints.

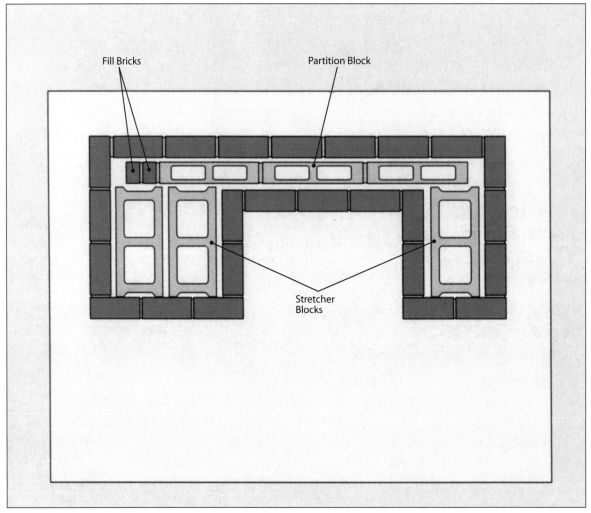

Fill Bricks

Partition Block

Stretcher Blocks

The pattern of bricks and blocks

The core of the barbecue consists of concrete blocks. In the two pedestals, stretcher blocks are laid directly atop each other, with vertical joints aligned, whereas the partition blocks at the back are laid in a running-bond pattern. Two bricks used for fill are mortared to one end of each course of partition blocks and are positioned at alternate ends to stagger the vertical joints. The block walls are not mortared to each other; the brick walls are anchored to the blocks with wall ties.

CONSTRUCTING THE BARBECUE

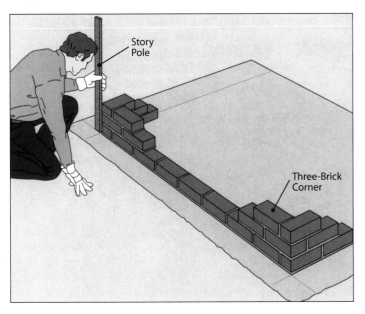

Story Pole

Three-Brick Corner

Starting the brick casing

Snap a chalk line for the back of the barbecue 6 inches from the edge of the slab. With a carpenter's square as a guide, chalk a perpendicular line 6 inches from one side of the slab. At the intersection of the lines, build a stepped three-brick corner. Check the brick height with a story pole *(page 158)*. Lay five more bricks to extend the first course along the back of the barbecue. Snap a third chalk line 6 inches from the other side of the slab, lay corner bricks along the line, then construct a second corner *(left)*. With a carpenter's square and a chalk line, outline the front of the barbecue and the firebox on the slab. Complete the first course of brick all around the barbecue and lay the second and third courses along the sides and back.

Starting the block core

Inside one of the pedestals, trowel just enough mortar onto the slab to form a bed for a stretcher block. Set a block on the mortar without displacing any bricks. Leave a ½-inch gap between the block and bricks. Lay two more blocks in the pedestals. Starting ½-inch from a back corner, set partition blocks along the back of the barbecue *(right)*. At the end of the course of partition blocks, set two bricks on end, mortaring them to the blocks as illustrated in the diagram on page 214. Check that the tops of the blocks are level with the top of the third brick course; adjust the thickness of the mortar beds under the blocks, if necessary.

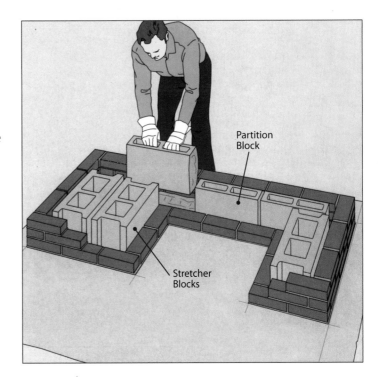

Partition Block

Stretcher Blocks

Wall Tie

Anchoring the bricks to the blocks

Lay the second and third courses of brick. Position wall ties every 10 inches across the blocks and bricks, placing them diagonally at the corners. Throw a mortar bed for a lead at one back corner of the barbecue. When you reach a tie, pick it up, apply the mortar (above), and reposition the tie, pushing it into the mortar. Repeat these steps until you've laid three courses of blocks. When applying the mortar for the blocks, bend the ties out of the way without disturbing the brick, lay the mortar, then bend the ties back into the mortar.

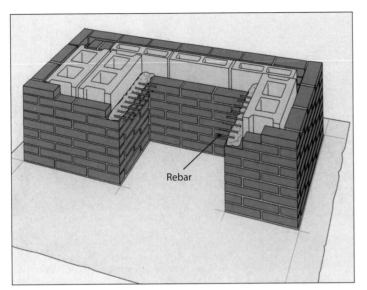

Rebar

Embedding supports for the ashpan and grate

Before completing the eighth and ninth brick courses, cut ⅜-inch rebar into pieces 7½ inches long with a hacksaw. For the ashpan, apply the mortar for the eighth course of firebox brick; then, push eight cut rebars at equal intervals into the mortar on each side of the firebox so they project beyond the brick by 4 inches as shown at left. Finish laying the eighth and ninth courses of bricks. For the grate, embed rebars in the mortar between the ninth and tenth courses of firebox brick, then finish the tenth and eleventh courses.

Laying props for the grill

Begin laying the twelfth course of brick—when you reach the insides of the firebox, butter one edge of each brick, rather than an end, and set it into the mortar so the opposite end projects beyond the bricks below by 4 inches. To steady the projecting bricks while the mortar is setting, weigh them down with bricks placed on end (right).

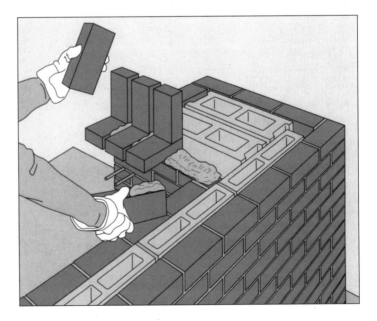

Trimming the joints

Once the mortar securing the projecting bricks has set for about 20 minutes, remove the weights and, with a ½-inch joint filler, rake excess mortar from the joints between them *(above)*. Position the last set of wall ties, then lay the thirteenth course of brick around the top of the barbecue.

Paving over the blocks

Lay a mortar bed on the fourth course of blocks. Fill in with a layer of brick laid in the pattern shown at right, buttering both ends and one side of each brick. Once the mortar is thumbprint hard, finish the joints.

Topping the barbecue

On one side of the barbecue top, place a large piece of cardboard, weigh it down, and outline as much of the top as possible on the underside of the cardboard *(right)*. Remove the cardboard, complete the outline with a straightedge, then cut along the lines to make a template. Reposition the template on the top and trim it flush with the edges. Make templates for the other side and the center section of the top. Trim ½ inch from each end of the center template to allow for mortar joints in the stone top. At a masonry-supply yard, have a piece of stone cut to match each template. Mortar them to the top of the barbecue. Let the mortar dry for two days, then coat the stone and its mortar joints with a resin-base stone-sealing compound to protect it from grease spatters.

Decorative Brick

Above all else, a brick wall is functional, but it can be made decorative by altering the traditional bonds, or patterns, in which bricks are laid, or by combining bricks of different colors.

A VARIETY OF LOOKS

The simplest way to achieve a decorative appearance is to cap a wall with specially cast coping bricks, or to tint the mortar. Also, the mortar joints can be finished with different tools to vary their shape, or left unfinished (page 22). These unfinished "weeping joints," however, will not withstand harsh climates.

Bricks can be offset to create an interplay of light and shadow, or to form a quoin—a design that accents a corner (pages 224–228). One decorative variant of brickwork is to make a lattice (pages 228–232); another is to create graceful serpentine curves (pages 233–239). Lattice and serpentine walls are laid in a single-brick thickness, and are generally no taller than 4 feet because of the consequent loss in strength. A serpentine wall in effect braces itself, but a lattice wall is buttressed every 6 to 10 feet with brick piers 12 to 16 inches square. For single-thickness walls, choose bricks with two finished faces. Tie the inner and outer walls of a double-thickness structure together with wall ties laid in the mortar every 12 inches along every second course.

PLANNING AHEAD

Any decorative brick wall requires a poured-concrete footing (pages 92–94). Check that your planned structure conforms to local building codes, and if the wall will rise near a property line, discuss your plans with your neighbor. To help with the ordering and setting of bricks, make a preliminary sketch on graph paper of one complete unit of the design, considering the variety of options for bricks.

TOOLS	MATERIALS
■ Mason's trowel	■ Mortar
■ Grapevine jointer	■ Bricks
■ Mason's ruler	■ Wall ties
■ Tuck pointer	
■ Mason's level	
■ Story pole	
■ Mason's line	
■ Line pins	
■ Chalk line	

SAFETY TIP

Protect your hands with gloves when working with mortar. Wear steel-toed shoes when handling bricks.

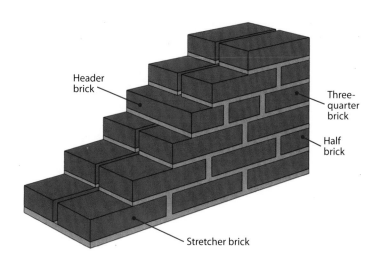

Header
brick

Three-quarter
brick

Half
brick

Stretcher brick

Bricklaying terms

The name given to a brick laid in a wall comes from its position. A stretcher brick is placed lengthwise, with its long narrow side forming the face of the wall. A brick laid crosswise with its ends facing outward is called a header brick. Courses of headers strengthen a double-thickness wall by binding the two layers together; for a single-thickness wall, you can substitute half bricks for the header courses. Half bricks and three-quarter bricks are also used to bring the courses even at the ends of walls.

GEOMETRIC DESIGNS

Common bond

Strong and easy to lay, common bond has a row of headers interrupting conventional rows of stretchers after every fifth course. Whole bricks, half bricks, or three-quarter bricks are laid at the ends of the wall as needed, in order to bring the courses even.

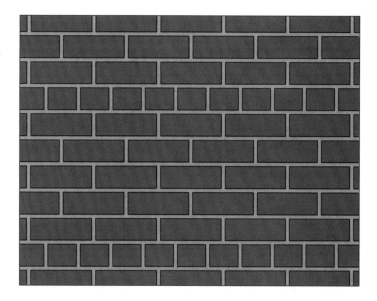

English bond

A decorative pattern that makes an exceptionally sturdy wall, English bond alternates courses of headers and stretchers.

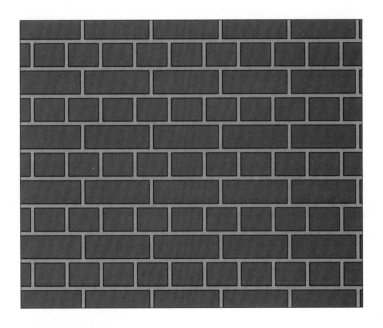

Flemish bond

Header bricks are alternated with stretcher bricks within each course in Flemish bond. As with common and English bonds, the strength of this wall is enhanced when the bricks are laid in this pattern.

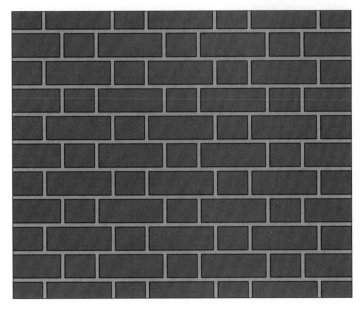

DESIGNS WITH COLOR

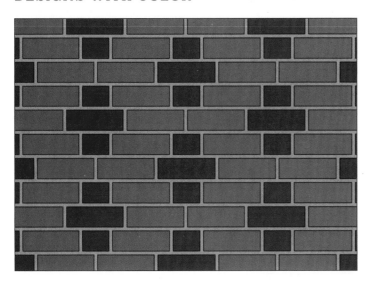

Flemish-cross bond

Standard Flemish courses alternate with courses consisting entirely of stretchers. Each of the headers in the Flemish course is color-contrasted with the stretchers in the same course, and aligned with every third brick in the stretchers-only course.

Flemish-spiral bond

This design bands the wall with diagonal lines of contrasting headers. Constructed of standard Flemish courses, the bricks are laid so that the headers in successive courses are staggered one half their width beyond the headers in the course below, with every course staggered in the same direction.

Garden-wall bond

Here, Flemish courses are modified, with three stretchers separating headers, to create a large diamond pattern. With each course, the row of contrasting bricks is lengthened by a half brick for five rows; each successive row is shortened by a half brick. For such dovetailing diamond patterns, a preliminary sketch helps you determine the proper placement of the header bricks that form the top, bottom, and center of each of the diamonds.

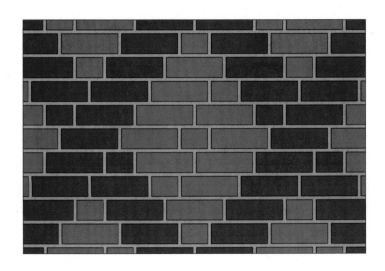

MORTAR JOINTS

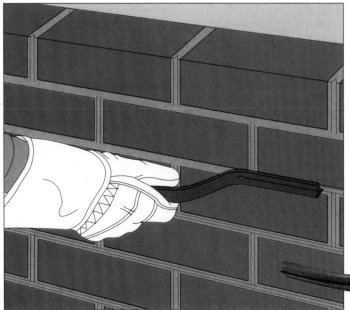

A grapevine joint

An hour or two after laying the bricks, fit a special ridged grapevine jointer *(photograph)* in the vertical mortar joints of your wall, pressing down firmly and drawing the jointer slowly along the mortar to create a narrow groove down the center. Tool the horizontal mortar joints in the same way *(left)*.

A weeping joint
Butter each brick with excess mortar. Press the bricks firmly into place, forcing out the mortar *(left)*, and taking care not to disturb the joints in the earlier courses. Allow the mortar that has squeezed out of the joints to cure undisturbed.

LAYING BRICKS IN RELIEF

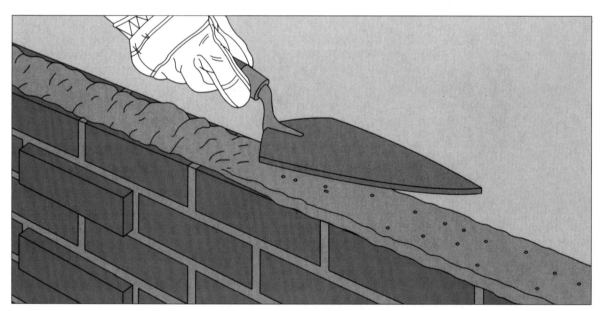

Mortaring
Throw a line of mortar along the course below the one where you will be laying projecting bricks, and pat the mortar flat with the back of your trowel *(above)*. Remove any mortar that spills over the edge of the course by trimming it away with the edge of the trowel. Lay the next course, positioning the offset bricks ⅝ inch—the width of a mason's rule—from the face of the wall, placing the rule beneath the brick as a guide. Build the wall up in this way, trimming the joints every course or two.

Trimming the joints
With a tuck pointer or a trowel, carefully trim all the joints around each offset brick flush with the surrounding bricks *(right)*. Finish all the other joints in the usual way.

AN OFFSET QUOIN

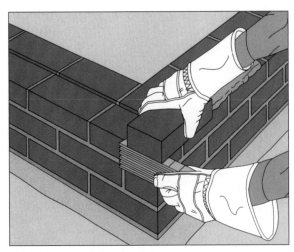

Laying the first offset course
Raise both the inner and outer walls to the height of the bottom of the planned quoin. At the corner, spread a bed of mortar long enough for two bricks along one outer wall—adding wall ties if necessary at this course as you would for a regular wall. Without furrowing the mortar, lay a corner brick so it is straddling the underlying vertical joint and offset from both faces of the wall by ⅝ inch—the width of a mason's ruler *(above, left)*. Lay a second

brick end to end with the first; check for horizontal alignment with a mason's level, first along the top of the bricks, then along their outer faces. Adjust the bricks if necessary by tapping them with a trowel handle. Lay a third brick at the corner, along the other wall *(above, right)*, setting it flush with the end of the first brick and checking its horizontal alignment. Check the height of the course of bricks using a story pole.

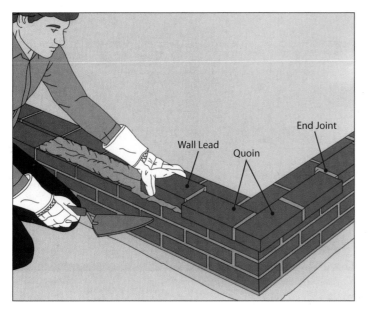

Completing the first course

Along the outer bricks of each wall, spread a mortar bed long enough for three or four bricks and furrow it. Lay the bricks flush with the face of the wall, making the end joints of these bricks slightly thicker than usual to compensate for the quoin's offset *(left)*. Check this flush course along both walls with a level and a story pole. Lay bricks along the inner walls at the corner, flush with the course below.

Building up the quoin

Lay a second course of offset bricks, positioning a half brick at the end of each leg so that the end bricks of the quoin line up with those underneath. Build the second course of the lead along both walls, beginning with half bricks and ending a half brick shorter than the first course *(right)*. Place a second course along the inner wall, setting the bricks flush with the wall surface. Lay courses of offset bricks until the quoin is the desired height—usually five courses—building up the lead on the outer and inner walls as you go, and setting wall ties at 12-inch intervals at every second course. Check the offset and flush bricks often for plumb and horizontal alignment; align each course with a story pole.

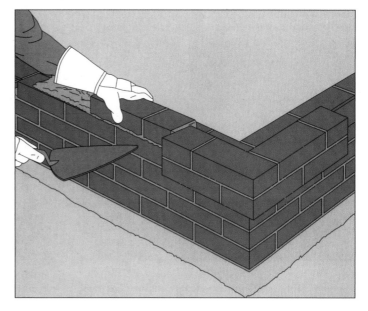

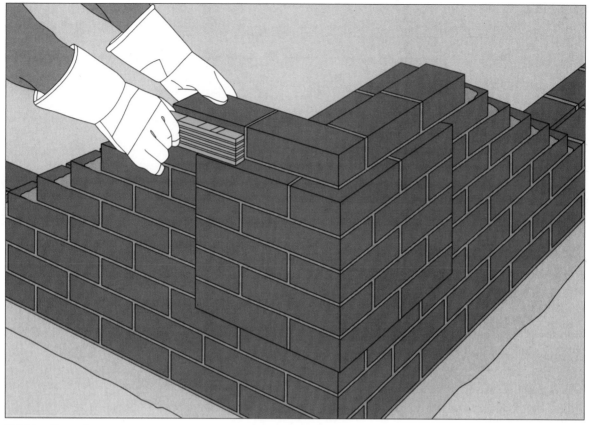

Finishing the quoin

At the top of the quoin, lay a course of bricks in nonfurrowed mortar flush with the face of the wall and ending a half brick short of the previous course *(above)*. Lay a second course of bricks in the same manner, but with furrowed mortar as for an ordinary wall. Raise up the inner wall to the level of these two courses. Build a lead, either quoined or conventional, at the opposite end of the wall.

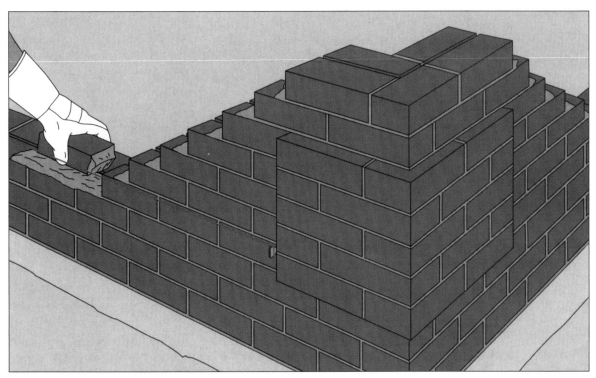

Filling in the wall

Run a mason's line along the first course of the leads, anchoring it near the quoins with line pins, and adjusting it to run even with the top of the course. To compensate for the wide end joint, space bricks evenly in a dry run from lead to lead. Spread mortar and reposition the bricks *(above)*, then lay a matching course along the inner wall. Reposition the mason's line along the top of the next course, and continue to raise the wall to the top of the lead, adding wall ties as required. Fill in holes left by line pins with fresh mortar as you work. Build up the adjacent wall in the same way.

Adding a second course

To start another quoin, lay a course of offset bricks as you did before. Following the brick pattern set by these two courses, build up the second quoin and its lead. Fill in the intervening wall. Continue building the walls in this way, alternating quoins with recessed courses until you reach the desired height *(right)*.

A MASONRY SCREEN

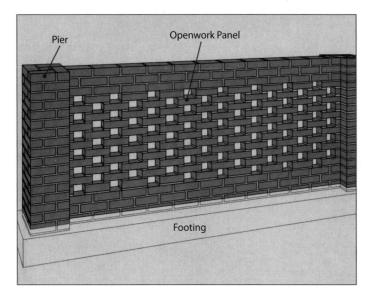

Pier

Openwork Panel

Footing

Anatomy of a latticework wall

This 18-foot screen, long enough to conceal a carport or to add privacy to a patio, consists of two openwork brick panels, each about 7½ feet long, buttressed by three brick piers, each 1 foot square. The panels, one brick thick, are banded top and bottom by three courses of solid brickwork, to frame the lattice and add stability. With eleven courses of latticework and six courses of solid brickwork, the wall is almost 4 feet high (because of the fragility of latticework masonry, it is best not to exceed this height). Check the local building code for the dimensions of the concrete footing; in this example it is 8 inches thick and 16 inches wide—allowing for 2 inches of clearance on either side of the piers—and it projects 2 inches beyond the ends of the piers.

ERECTING BRICK LATTICE

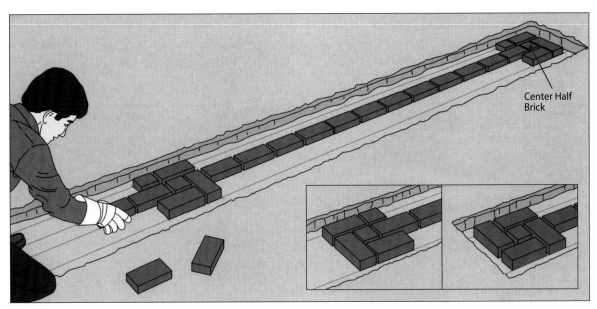

Center Half Brick

Beginning the latticework

Snap two chalk lines along the footing, 12 inches apart, to mark the outer faces of the piers, then snap a second pair of lines, 4 inches in from each pier line and 4 inches apart, to mark the outer faces of the panels. With a crayon, measure off and mark the points where the piers will cross the panel lines. Lay bricks in a dry run, beginning with an end pier, pinwheeling the bricks around a center half brick so that the first brick of the wall panel intersects the pier. Continue placing unmortared bricks between the chalk lines to the middle pier, spacing mortar joints so the last brick falls either a mortar joint away from the pier mark or halfway across it. If the last brick falls a mortar joint away from the pier mark, the pier pattern will follow the one in the illustration above and the right inset; if it falls halfway across the pier mark, it will follow the design in the left inset. Add a half brick and pinwheel the remaining bricks making up the middle pier. Repeat this procedure to position the bricks for the second panel and the third pier; the pier's pattern will depend on whether the last panel brick ends outside the pier or within it.

Laying the solid bands

Lay the first course of each pier in mortar, as well as the first two lead bricks at each end of one of the panels. Check the thickness of the mortar bed with a story pole, and the horizontal alignment of the bricks with a mason's level or a 4-foot-long carpenter's level. Lay two more courses on the piers and the panel leads, alternating the arrangement of bricks on the pier so the first brick of each panel lead steps back by a half brick from the underlying course *(above)*; check your work frequently for alignment, plumb, and course level.

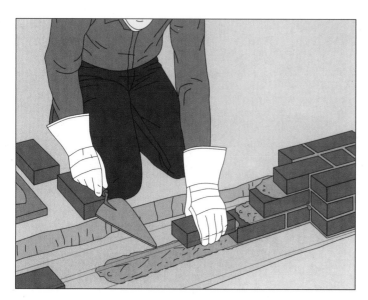

Completing the bands

Stretch a mason's line flush with the top of the first course, setting line pins in the mortar joints to hold it in place. Fill in the intermediate bricks, removing three or four dry-run bricks at a time and replacing them in mortar *(left)*. Lay the next two courses, moving up the mason's line as you go and patching the holes left by the line pins with fresh mortar. Repeat the process to lay the solid bands for the second panel.

Beginning the latticework

At the fourth course, set the pier bricks dry; if the pier is intersected by a panel brick, cut the intersecting brick by 2 inches *(inset)*. Working from two piers toward the center, lay a dry run of panel bricks, about 4 inches apart and spaced evenly *(above)*. Set the pier bricks in mortar, then remove and set the first three or four lead bricks at each end of the panel, laying a mortar bed that is no longer than each of the bricks; remove any excess mortar. Check the lead for vertical alignment with a story pole and for horizontal alignment with a level.

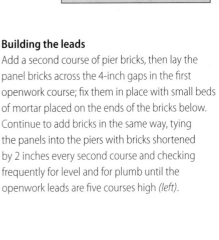

Intersecting Brick

Building the leads

Add a second course of pier bricks, then lay the panel bricks across the 4-inch gaps in the first openwork course; fix them in place with small beds of mortar placed on the ends of the bricks below. Continue to add bricks in the same way, tying the panels into the piers with bricks shortened by 2 inches every second course and checking frequently for level and for plumb until the openwork leads are five courses high *(left)*.

Filling in the latticework

Stretch a mason's line flush with the top of the first course of the openwork leads, and set the remaining bricks in the course *(right)*. Raise the line to match the second course of the leads and fill in the openwork, centering the bricks over the 4-inch gaps in the first course. Continue in this way until the latticework is even with the tops of the leads. Raise the second openwork panel to an equal height in the same way. With a tuck pointer, trim away any mortar that has squeezed into the open spaces *(inset)*. Continue the latticework upward, building six-course leads, then filling in the openwork; trim away any mortar in the open spaces. Patch the holes left by the line pins.

Capping the screen

Lay a dry run of a new course of solid brickwork along the top of the panels. Adjust the spacing of the mortar joints so that they are even, then build three-course leads of solid brickwork; take care not to spill the mortar into the open spaces of the latticework as you lay mortar for the first course of the leads. Check the leads frequently for plumb and level and, with a story pole, make sure the three courses are of uniform thickness. Fill in the solid brickwork between the leads, with a mason's line as a guide *(left)*.

A Serpentine Wall

With its unusual complexities of design, a serpentine wall adds grace and charm to its surroundings. Repeated S curves, rather than frequent piers and a double thickness of bricks, give this wall stability.

DESIGN

The S curves are a succession of arcs, each an identical segment from a circle of a given radius. The arcs are linked end to end in mirror image down the length of the wall and are terminated by a brick pier at each end of the wall. Since the proportions of the arcs determine the structure's inherent strength, make sure that the radius of the arcs is no greater than twice the height of the wall, and that the total sweep of the arcs from side to side covers a distance equal to at least half the height of the wall.

FOOTINGS

A concrete footing *(pages 92–94)*, 8 inches thick and resting below the frost line, is adequate. Usually you can dig a simple trench 16 inches wide and 4 inches longer than the wall, but in sandy soil you may need to build curved forms *(page 69)*. For clayey or boggy ground, consult a professional.

SPECIAL TECHNIQUES

Most of the standard bricklaying techniques are employed in building this wall, but since the curves make it impossible for you to use stepped leads and a mason's line to align the courses, you will need to use other methods to check the courses for plumb, level, and proper curve. A plywood template ensures that the curves are identical *(pages 235–236)*. Parallel string lines are set up to mark the outer sweep of the curves, and these strings also serve to plumb and level the courses as you construct the wall *(pages 236–239)*.

TOOLS	MATERIALS
■ Maul	■ Stakes
■ Saber saw	■ 2 × 2s, 2 × 4s
■ Wheelbarrow	■ Plywood (½")
■ Square shovel	■ String
■ Float	■ Picture wire
■ Carpenter's square	■ Powdered chalk
■ Level	■ Concrete
■ Story pole	■ Bricks
■ Mason's trowel	■ Mortar
	■ Corrugated-steel wall ties

SAFETY TIP

Put on hard-toed shoes and gloves when handling bricks. Wear long sleeves when applying mortar.

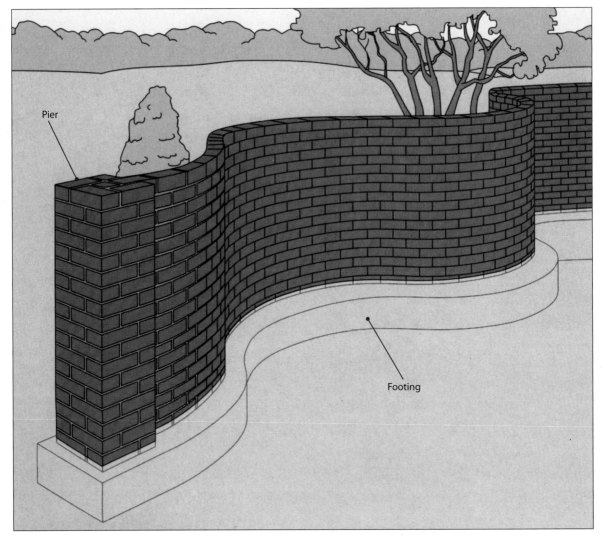

Anatomy of a serpentine wall

This traditional serpentine wall consists of one thickness of bricks, built to a height of 4 feet. Each of its undulating curves is a segment of a circle with a radius of 6 feet. The distance between two parallel lines touching the outermost points of the curves is 39½ inches, which includes the width of the bricks. On each side of the wall, the distance between the outermost points of successive curves is 15 feet 10 inches. Brick piers 12 inches square fortify the ends of the wall, and steel wall ties running from brick to brick along every fifth course provide additional strength. Just below ground level, the wall rests on a similarly curved concrete footing; in this example, it is 16 inches wide, 8 inches thick, and extends 2 inches beyond the wall at each end.

LAYING THE GROUNDWORK

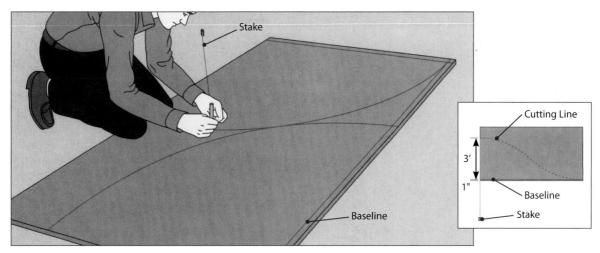

Tracing the template

Mark a baseline 1 inch from one of the long edges of a 4- by 8-foot sheet of ½-inch plywood. Drive a stake into the ground as the center point of a circle and tie one end of a length of picture wire to it. Measure out 6 feet of wire from the stake and twist it around a felt-tipped marker. Position the plywood so the wire, stretched along one end of the sheet, extends 3 feet past the baseline; with the wire taut, draw an arc across the plywood to mark the first part of the cutting line *(inset)*. Reverse the plywood and mark a line 1 inch from the end, then adjust the sheet so the wire runs along this line. Beginning at the baseline, draw an arc toward the center of the sheet, extending the curve until the two arcs touch *(above)*. With a saber saw, cut along both arcs, starting at the end of one arc and switching to the other arc at the point where the two touch. Cut off the 1 inch marked on the far edge where you began the second arc.

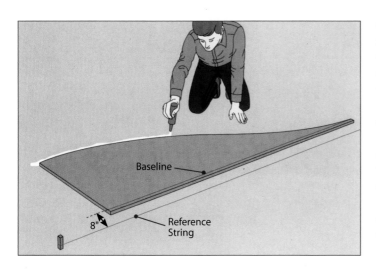

Outlining one side of the footing trench
Stretch a reference string slightly longer than the planned wall along a line representing the outermost curves of one face of the wall. Secure the ends of the string to two stakes so it lies about 1 inch above the ground. Lay the template at one end of the planned wall, with the baseline positioned half the width of the planned footing away from the string—in this case, 8 inches. Outline the curved edge of the template with powdered chalk *(left)*. Turn the template end over end, mark a baseline 1 inch in from the edge on the other side, and repeat the process to mark off the remaining curves on that side of the planned footing.

Completing the outline

Position the template's baseline half the footing width away from the other side of the reference string and outline a parallel serpentine line *(right)*. The two curved lines represent the full width of the footing. Extend the curved lines at each end with straight, parallel lines about 14 inches long for the pier footings. Remove the reference string and dig a footing trench between the lines. Pour a footing *(pages 92–94)*, and allow it to cure for at least 24 hours before beginning to lay bricks for the wall.

16"

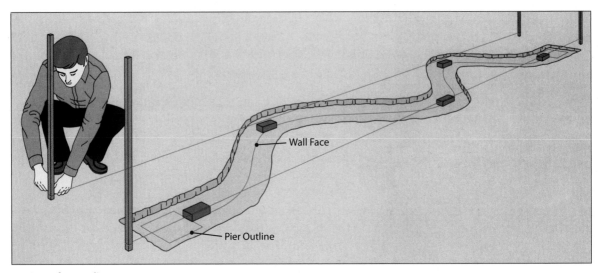

Wall Face

Pier Outline

Setting reference lines

With a carpenter's square, outline a 12-inch-square pier 2 inches from each end of the footing. Position the template near one end of the footing so its curved edge is offset from the middle of the footing by the width of a brick. Outline one wall face on the footing, turning the template over, and marking the outline with a crayon rather than chalk. Stretch a string 4 feet longer than the planned wall along the footing so it touches the outermost curves of the crayon line on one face of the wall. Drive a 2-by-2 as tall as the wall into the ground 2 feet past each end of the footing, plumb it, and tie on the string. Stretch a second string across the footing, parallel to the first and 39½ inches away from it. Place bricks along the crayon line at each end and at the outermost points of the curves to check that the strings are even with the edges of the bricks. Tie the second string to stakes *(above)*, marking the other face of the wall.

RAISING THE WALL

Laying a dry run

With a story pole as a guide, raise the two strings between the reference poles to a height one course above the footing. Lay a course of bricks—without mortar—inside one pier outline, pin-wheeling the bricks around a center half brick (page 229). Position a dry run of bricks down the middle of the footing, aligning the bricks with the crayon line and setting them ⅜ inch apart to allow for mortar joints (left). Adjust the spacing between the last few bricks so the final unit either falls a mortar joint short of the pier outline or crosses the outline at its midpoint, as for a brick lattice (page 229). Lay a dry course of bricks for the second pier, cutting a brick if necessary to interlock with the wall.

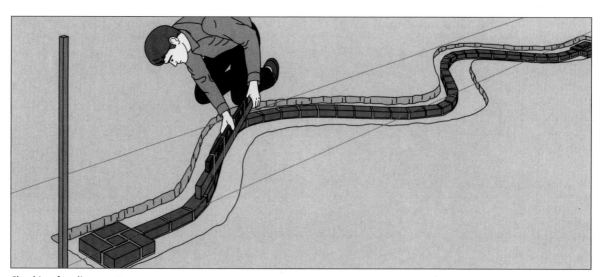

Checking for alignment

Mortar the first course of bricks for the pier. Remove three or four bricks at a time along the length of the dry run, then mortar them in place. Check that the tops of the outermost bricks along each curve align with the reference strings. Check the intermediate bricks for level by spanning a section of curve with a 2-by-4 topped by a level secured with tape. Position the board with one end resting on an outermost brick and pivot it (above). To bring bricks into alignment, tap them with a trowel handle to lower them; or remove them and add more mortar to raise them. Lay the bricks for the other pier in mortar.

CHAPTER 4: BUILDING WITH BRICK, BLOCK, TILE, AND STONE

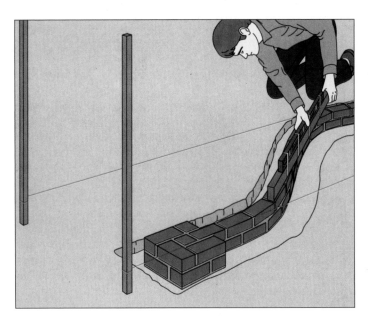

Laying the second course

Add a second course of bricks, moving the reference strings to the new course level. At the piers, arrange the bricks so their vertical joints are at the midpoint of the bricks in the course below and the first brick that extends into the wall crosses the midpoint of the brick below. Check for alignment *(left)*, and make any necessary adjustments.

Checking the curves

After laying the second course, set the plywood template into the curves of the brickwork, supporting it with bricks at the level of the second course; look down onto the template to make sure that each end touches a brick at the outermost points of the curve. Bring the intermediate bricks into alignment by tapping them with the trowel handle until they lie flat against the template's curved edge *(right)*. Check along the length of the wall, flipping the template as necessary to match the curves. Check the other curves along the second course in the same way.

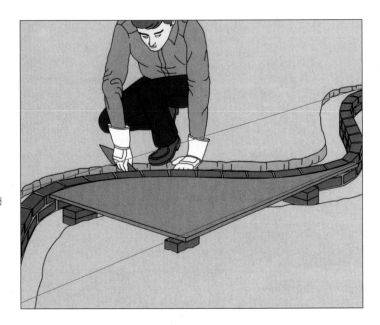

Adding to the brickwork

Raise the wall to the fifth course, resetting the string lines and checking each completed course for level, plumb, and correct curvature. Throw the mortar for the sixth course, then set a corrugated-steel wall tie across each vertical joint. Continue raising the wall *(above)*, setting ties at every fifth course. As the wall rises, you may need to stand on a stepladder and have a pair of helpers hold the template level against the course of bricks while you check the curvature.

Building Brick Arches

Designed to support the masonry above wall openings, arches are built for their beauty as much as for structural purposes. The two most common styles are the semicircular and the jack, or flat *(opposite)*.

DESIGN AND CONSTRUCTION

For an arch to be self-supporting, its face must be at least as high as the thickness of the wall surrounding it, and its depth must equal that thickness. Although an arch can span more than 5 feet, such a project is best left to a professional. During construction, a semicircular arch is supported on temporary shoring referred to as a buck, which serves as a template while the bricks are being laid and carries the load until the mortar sets. Jack arches can be built to be self-supporting, but they are usually placed on permanent steel lintels. Buy a lintel that extends beyond the opening at least 8 inches on either side.

SHAPED BRICKS

If you build the arch with standard bricks, you will have to taper the mortar joints between them to fit. An alternative is to buy specially shaped bricks from a masonry supplier. Such bricks generally cost more, but they produce a better-looking arch. And in a jack arch, each brick is a slightly different size, so it is best to buy them ready-made. When ordering shaped bricks, supply the dealer with a full-size drawing of the arch, and plan the project well in advance since it will take some time for the shipment to arrive.

TOOLS	MATERIALS
■ Hammer	■ 2 x 4s
■ Saber saw	■ Plywood (¼," ½")
■ Mason's tape	■ Common nails (3")
■ Level	■ Double-headed nails (3½")
■ Mason's trowel	
■ Mason's line	■ Masonry nails (3½")
■ Jointer	■ Roofing nails (1")
■ Circular saw with masonry blade	■ Picture wire
	■ Bricks
■ Bricklayer's hammer	■ Mortar
■ Pointing chisel	■ Jack-arch brick kit
■ Maul	■ Steel lintel (¼" x 3½" x 3½")
■ Mason's hawk	
■ Joint filler	■ Polyethylene sheeting (6-mil)
	■ Corrugated-steel wall ties

SAFETY TIP

Put on hard-toed shoes to protect your feet from falling bricks, and wear work gloves when handling bricks and working with mortar. Don goggles to drive nails or operate a power tool.

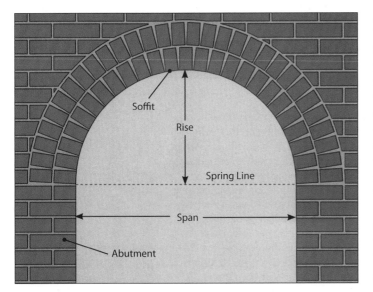

A semicircular arch

This type of arch consists of two rings of standard-size bricks laid on edge. For the bricks to follow the curve of the arch, the mortar joints are made slightly wedge shaped—thicker at the top than at the bottom. Because the outside ring follows a wider radius than the inside ring, it requires a greater number of bricks. The ends of the arch rest on masonry walls referred to as abutments; for this type of arch, the abutments are two bricks thick. The imaginary horizontal line between the points where the arch meets the abutments is called the spring line. The distance between the abutments is the span, and the rise of the arch is the vertical distance from the spring line to the center of the underside of the arch. The entire underside of the arch is known as the soffit.

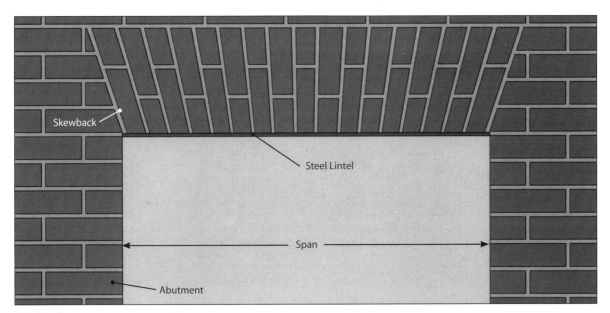

A jack arch

Every brick in a jack, or flat, arch is cut to a slightly different shape, because each one sits at a slightly different angle to the steel lintel that supports it. The angle of the skewback—the inclined surfaces of the side walls, or abutments—is generally 70 degrees. When ordering a set of bricks for a jack arch, specify the span of the opening, the thickness of the mortar joints, and the height of the arch in terms of horizontal courses of surrounding brick (four, in this example). Other specifications are the depth of the arch and the pattern of the brickwork in the face of the arch—a running bond in this case.

FORMING A SEMICIRCULAR OPENING

Spring Line

Shaping the buck

On a sheet of ½-inch plywood, draw a spring line for the arch several inches in from the edge. Drive a nail at the center of the line and link a pencil to the nail with a piece of picture wire half the length of the spring line. Swing the pencil around to draw an arc connecting the ends of the spring line (above). At each end of the spring line, continue the line straight to the edge of the plywood. Then, with a saber saw, cut along this line and around the arc. Using the cut plywood as a pattern, cut a matching piece. Nail a 2-by-4 spacer block on edge along the spring line between the two plywood pieces. Add shorter 2-by-4 spacers at intervals around the curved edge, fanning out from the center like the spokes of a wheel.

Marking brick positions

Lay the buck on the ground. Place one brick on end exactly at the center on top of the arch. Fill one side of the arch, spacing the bricks about ⅜ inch apart and with the last brick ⅜ inch above the spring line. Adjust the bricks if necessary, and check that the spacing is even by bending a mason's tape around the curve of the buck. Fill in the other side of the arch with the same number of bricks *(left)*. Mark all the brick positions on the face of the buck. Arrange a second ring of bricks around the first, starting ⅜ inch above the spring line, leaving a ⅜-inch gap between rings, and spacing the bricks evenly. Record the width at both ends of the wedge-shaped gaps between adjacent bricks.

Spring Line

Setting up the buck

Hold the buck in place in the arch opening with the spring line level with the tops of the abutments, while a helper measures the distance between the spring-line spacer block and the ground. Cut two 2-by-4 legs to this length. Check the length of the legs by propping up the buck with each leg supporting one end of the spring-line spacer block. With 3½-inch double-headed nails, fasten the legs in place between the plywood faces of the buck. Cut two 2-by-4 crosspieces equal in length to the span of the arch. Nail a crosspiece to one side of the pair of legs *(right)*. Turn the assembly over and nail a crosspiece to the other side of the legs. Raise the buck into the opening, hold a carpenter's level across the bottom edges of the two plywood pieces and, if necessary, slide shims beneath the legs to make the buck sit perfectly level. If the buck tends to tip, drive a masonry nail through each leg into mortar joints at the sides of the opening.

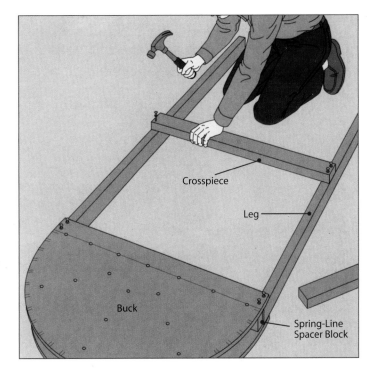

Crosspiece

Leg

Buck

Spring-Line
Spacer Block

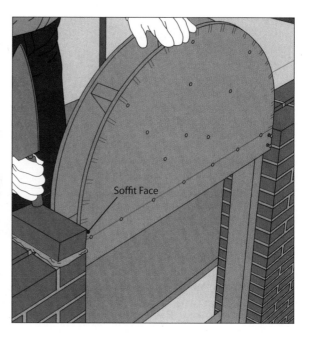

Soffit Face

Beginning the first ring

Set up a mason's line level with the top of the first brick in the arch. Load a mason's trowel with mortar and shake the blade sharply downward. Then apply mortar along one bed of a brick, beveling the mortar so that there is a smaller amount on the part of the bed that will face in the direction of the opening (above, left). Lay the brick atop the corner of the abutment with its soffit face resting

squarely against the buck. With the handle of the trowel, tamp the brick into the mortar (above, right) until it fits precisely between the marks on the buck, with its end flush with the mason's line. Continue laying bricks on both sides of the buck in this manner, raising the mason's line for each brick, until you reach the marks that you made on the buck to position the center brick.

A GUIDE FOR ANGLED BRICKS

The trick to creating a strong and even arch is to place each brick at the correct angle. This can be done by eye, but an easier and more accurate method is to use a guide. Cut a straight 1-by-2 slightly longer than the rise of the arch and nail one end at the center point of the spring line on the buck. As you place each brick, swing the stick around until it rests against the exposed edge of the brick. Adjust the angle of the brick until it matches the angle of the stick.

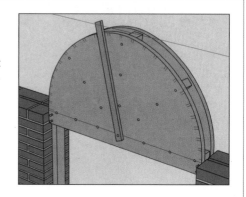

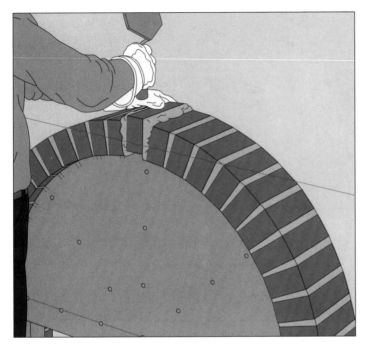

Laying the center brick

Butter the beds of both bricks adjoining the center brick. Butter the center brick on both beds. Slide the brick into place, tapping it with the trowel handle to wedge it against the buck *(left)*. When the mortar has hardened enough to retain a thumbprint, tool all of the joints that will be visible on the completed arch as you would for the horizontal courses of the wall.

Building the outside ring

Butter one bed of a brick. Also spread mortar on the brick face that will lie against the inside ring. Lay the brick in place on top of one abutment, tapping it into the mortar until there is a ⅜-inch joint between the end of this brick and the adjoining one in the first ring. Lay a few more bricks in the same way, creating wedge-shaped mortar joints following your measurements. When you are partway up the curve of the arch, spread mortar along the top of the inside ring; continue laying bricks, buttering only one bed of each unit *(right)*. When you reach the middle of the arch, do not lay the center brick; build up the other side of the arch in the same way, and then lay the center brick.

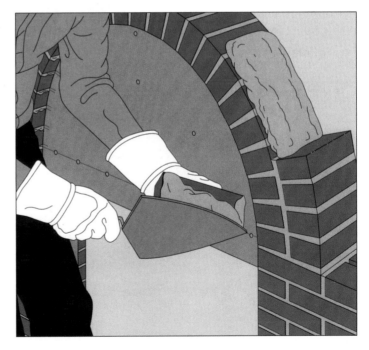

Continuing the wall upward

Fill in horizontal courses of masonry on one side of the arch. When you get too close to the arch to fit a full brick, mark the outside face of a brick for a diagonal cut. Score the marked line ½ inch deep with a circular saw fitted with a masonry blade; then finish the cut by chipping away the waste portion of the brick with the blade end of a bricklayer's hammer. Alternatively, make the cut with a masonry saw. Butter the ends of the cut brick and slip it into place. Continue raising courses on both sides, cutting bricks as necessary to fit them against the arch *(right)*, until the arch is fully enclosed. Finish the joints.

Finishing the arch

After the mortar has cured for about five days, remove the pieces bracing the legs of the buck. With a helper supporting the buck, remove the nails fastening the legs and pry the bottoms of the 2-by-4s toward the center of the opening. Ease the buck out from under the arch. With a pointing chisel and a maul, cut out the hardened mortar from the joints of the soffit *(above)*, clearing them to a depth of ½ inch. Load a hawk or the back of a trowel with mortar and hold it up close to the cleared joints. Force the mortar into the joints with a joint filler, packing them completely. When the mortar has set enough to hold a thumbprint, finish the soffit joints to match those on the face of the arch.

SETTING A JACK ARCH

Making the pattern
From a piece of ¼-inch plywood, cut a full-size pattern of the planned arch. Taking care to arrange the arch bricks in the same configuration in which they were shipped, lay all the bricks in place on the pattern, leaving spaces for mortar joints between the bricks and at either end of the pattern *(left)*. Mark the positions of the mortar-joint gaps along the top and bottom edges of the pattern. Remove the bricks, again setting them down in exactly the order in which they were assembled.

Framing the arch
For the first course above the spring line, lay the end bricks no closer than 8 inches from the sides of the opening. Continue raising courses, offsetting each succeeding course one half brick back *(right)*, until you have reached the planned height of the arch on both sides of the opening. Install a steel lintel and polyethylene flashing. Fill the space between the front edge of the lintel and the face of the bricks in the abutments by scraping a little mortar off a trowel onto the front edge of the lintel on both sides of the opening.

Positioning the bricks

Lay several bricks mortarless and ⅜ inches apart on the lintel—enough bricks so that when the successive, stepped-back courses are laid, their ends will extend far enough over the top of the opening to be covered by the plywood pattern when held above the opening. Lay a mortar bed for the next course, but leave the vertical joints free of mortar, and step the course a half brick back from the center of the opening. Build each successive course in this way, until you reach a height equal to that of the plywood pattern *(right)*. Position bricks on the opposite side of the opening in the same way.

Marking the skewback angle

Align the bottom of the plywood pattern with the top edge of the lintel, and center the pattern in the opening. Follow the sides of the pattern with a pencil to mark the skewback bricks *(left)*; then mark the bricks on the other end of the pattern. Number the marked bricks from bottom to top, then remove all of these bricks; scrape off any mortar adhering to their surfaces. Cut the marked bricks on the diagonal.

Building the skewbacks

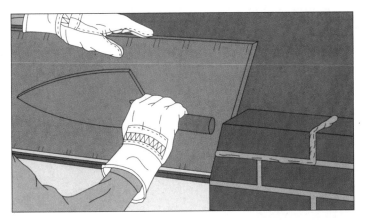

With the plywood pattern resting on the lintel, lay the numbered cut bricks in their original positions but this time with mortar; tamp each brick into the mortar until it fits flush against the edge of the pattern *(left)*. Transfer the joint marks on the pattern to the backup wall behind the arch and to the front lip of the steel lintel with chalk. Stretch a mason's line even with the tops of the skewbacks.

Beginning the arch

Butter one side of the bottom corner brick of the arch, with only a little mortar on the bottom part that will rest on the lintel *(right)*. Lay the brick in place against the skewback and tamp it into the mortar with the handle of the trowel until it is lined up with the marks on the lintel. Spread mortar on the top end of this first brick, then butter the half brick that fits on top of it; tamp the half brick in place, aligning its top with the mason's line and its sides with the marks on the backup wall. Install the first two bricks at the other end of the arch in the same way.

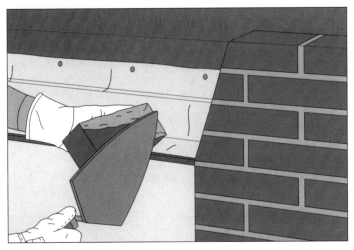

Completing the job

Working from both sides toward the center fill in all the remaining arch bricks—except the center ones—in their correct order, paying close attention to the thickness of the mortar joints *(left)*. Butter the center bricks on both sides and tap them into place with the handle of the trowel. Continue building the wall above the arch; to reinforce the top of the arch, lay a row of wall ties, end to end, in the mortar bed laid for the first course of bricks above the arch.

Constructing Stone Arches

Whether spanning windows, doors, or fireplaces, or resting on a pair of piers to frame an entryway, stone arches lend a touch of timelessness to any setting.

PLANNING AHEAD

The principles and procedures for building a stone arch are very similar to those for brick arches *(pages 240–249)*; however, the work is more exacting, and will probably require a helper on scaffolding on the other side of the wall as well, to position the heavier stones. Since a stone arch is only as strong as its abutments and footing, the wall footing *(pages 92–94)* must continue along the opening, and the mortar in the abutments themselves—whether they are freestanding piers or walls—needs to set at least 24 hours before arch stones are laid. The piers for an arch that is not part of a larger wall—as well as the arch itself—need to be at least 12 inches thick.

A stone arch, like a stone wall, requires a stiff mortar mixture, and the stones themselves must be strong, weather resistant, and workable—since you will need to do a lot of precise shaping *(pages 188–189)*. Single stones the thickness of the wall produce the strongest arch. However, smaller stones can also make up the required thickness, or be combined to make an arch slightly thicker than the wall, as a way of highlighting the arch. If you want to ensure precision, you can take your stone and a template of the arch to a professional stonemason to have the cuts made.

BRACING THE ARCH

The buck for a stone arch serves the same purpose as the one used for a brick arch. But because of the great weight of the stone, wooden shims are used to wedge the buck into place and, after the arch is built, they are pulled out to relieve the compression on the supports to allow the removal of the buck.

TOOLS		MATERIALS
■ Handsaw	■ Pointing trowel	■ 2 x 4s, 4 x 4s
■ Saber saw	■ Stiff-bristle brush	■ Plywood (½")
■ Hammer		■ Hardboard (¼")
■ Maul	■ Level	■ Shims
■ Stone chisel	■ T-bevel	■ Double-headed nails (3½")
■ Stone hammer	■ Tuck pointer	
■ Pitching tool	■ Pointing chisel	■ Common nails (1", 3½")
■ Bricklayer's hammer	■ Joint filler	■ Stones
■ Mason's trowel		■ Mortar

SAFETY TIP

Put on work gloves when working with mortar, and add hard-toed shoes when handling stone. Wear goggles to use power tools, to drive nails, and to cut stone.

PEAKED ARCH

Skewback Stone

Lintels

Footing

Abutments

SEMICIRCULAR ARCH

Keystone

Abutments

Footing

Two types of arches

A peak *(above, left)* and a semicircle *(above, right)* are two common designs for stone arches. The peaked arch, built over a triangular buck, has two paving stones that act as lintels and rest against skewback stones topping each abutment *(pages 252–255)*. The semicircular arch is made by setting large tapered stones over a semicircular buck; a keystone fits into position at the center *(page 257)*.

BUILDING A PEAK

Setting up the buck

Cut a triangle from ½-inch plywood, with the base
equal to the distance between the abutments and
the distance to the peak equal to the desired rise
from the base. Make another identical triangle; then,
join the two with 2-by-4 spacers 2 inches shorter
than the wall thickness. Trim four 4-by-4 posts
½ inch shorter than the height of the spring line.
For each pair of posts, cut 2-by-4 spacers so that
the assembly will be 1 inch narrower than the
thickness of the wall, and toenail them to the posts
at the top and bottom as well as every few feet in
between with 3½-inch common nails. To join the
assemblies, cut 2-by-4s long enough to hold them
firmly in place against the abutments, then toenail
these spreaders to the top and bottom of each post.
Position the buck on top of the post assembly,
then tap in a wooden shim over each post *(right)*;
continue tapping in one and then the other until
the buck is at the spring line and level. With 3½-inch
double-headed nails, toenail up through the tops of
the posts, through the shims, and into the buck.

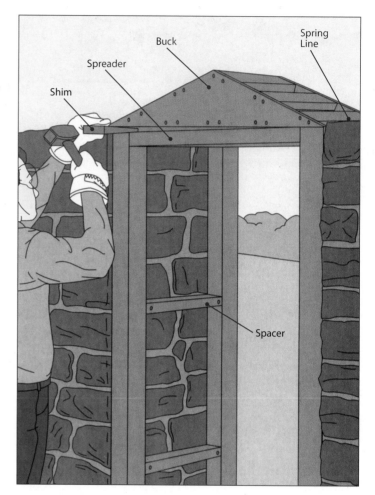

Setting the skewback stones

Select or cut stones that span the width of each abutment, trimming one side of each stone (pages 188–189) to form an approximate right angle with the top surface of the buck. Lay the first skewback stone in a ¾-inch bed of mortar, with its angled end 1 inch away from the abutment edge (above), then lay the opposite skewback stone in the same way. About an hour after the skewback stones have been laid, tool their wall-face joints, then let the mortar set for at least 24 hours.

Mitering the lintel stones

Measure the distance from the peak of the buck to the bottom of the skewback stones, then select two paving stones for the lintels, each a few inches longer than this measurement and at least 4 inches thick. Subtract ¾ inch from the measurement to allow for mortar joints at each end and mark this length on one paving stone. Repeat this measuring and marking procedure for the paving stone on the other side of the arch. Holding a level perpendicular to the base of the buck, extend it past the buck's peak and set the arms of a T-bevel flush with the buck and the level *(above)*; mark this angle on the stones. Cut the stones, taking care not to make them too short. Lay the lintels in place on top of the buck to check their fit, then remove and trim them if necessary.

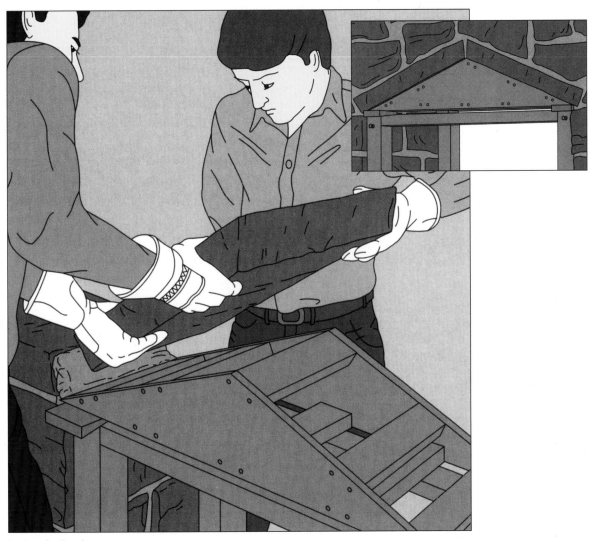

Laying the lintels

Throw a ¾-inch bed of mortar on the angled side of one skewback stone. Dampen the first lintel with water and, with a helper, lower it into place *(above)*, sliding it down until the end rests in the mortar, and shifting it from side to side to center it; press it against the mortar until the joint is ½ inch thick. Set the other lintel in the same way. Tamp mortar into the joint at the peak with a ½-inch tuck pointer; allow the mortar to set for at least 24 hours. Build the wall in level courses over the arch, beveling the stones adjacent to the lintel for a close fit *(inset)*. Remove the shims and buck after 10 days, then repoint the joints on the underside of the lintel by first cutting and refilling them and then tooling

CREATING A HALF-ROUND PORTAL

Building the buck

Make a semicircular buck *(page 242)* but using the edge of the plywood as the spring line and making it ½ inch less than the span between the abutments; join the two pieces of plywood together with 2-by-4 spacers 2 inches shorter than the wall thickness. Cut a strip of 5-inch hardboard as wide as the thickness of the buck. Nail the hardboard over the arch of the buck with 1-inch nails, starting at one end and bending the hardboard gently as you fasten it to the edges of the plywood *(right)*; at the opposite end, cut away any excess hardboard. Cut a marking string about 18 inches longer than the radius of the arch, lay the buck on its side, and attach the string to the nail used to draw the semicircle.

Positioning the stones

Select similarly sized stones as thick as the wall for the ends of the arch. Position a stone flush against the arch at each end of the buck. If it doesn't lie flat against the buck, scratch a line on it parallel to the edge of the buck with a tuck pointer. Pull the marking string over the the form's spring line and scratch a cutting line on the end of the stone. Mark the other edge of the stone in the same way—drawing a corresponding line on the buck—then mark both edges of the other stone *(left)*. Remove the stones and cut along the scribed lines *(page 126)*. Using the lines on the buck as references, leave ½- to ¾-inch gaps for mortar joints and mark the bottom edges of a second pair of stones. Continue marking and cutting pairs of stones on opposite sides of the buck, working toward the top; mark their positions on the buck and allow for a single keystone at the top. Number the stones to indicate their positions for assembly.

Marking String

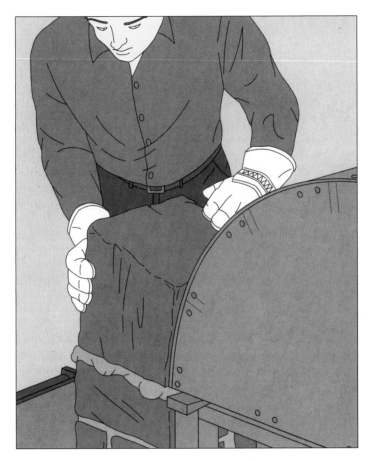

Laying the stones

Set up the buck on a post assembly in the opening, then lay a ¾-inch bed of mortar on one abutment. Dampen the first stone slightly and center it on the mortar bed, twisting or rocking it lightly until it presses the mortar to a ½-inch joint. Remove the excess mortar with a trowel. Set a stone on the opposite abutment in the same manner. Lay successive pairs of stones until only the gap for the keystone remains.

Setting the keystone

Butter both sides of the stones adjoining the keystone with mortar, then butter both sides of the keystone. Slide the keystone into the space at the top of the arch, centering it carefully. Finish all visible joints, striking them to match the depth of the joints in the abutments. Allow the mortar to cure for 10 days, then remove the buck. Repoint the underside of the arch, by first cutting a ½-inch recess at each joint, then finishing the joints to match the rest of the arch.

Index

Index

Index

Landscaping

The DIY Guide to Planning, Planting, and Building a Better Yard

By Skills Institute Press

From growing lawns and planting trees, to putting in stone walkways or water elements, readers will discover the right way to do it in straight-forward steps that anyone can follow to realize their dreams.

ISBN: 978-1-56523-699-8
$24.95 • 288 Pages

Weatherproofing

The DIY Guide to Keeping Your Home Warm in the Winter, Cool in the Summer, and Dry All Year Around

By Skills Institute Press

Whether you need to add insulation in your attic or weather-strip your doors, this book has the details that you need to keep your home comfortable year round.

ISBN: 978-1-56523-591-5
$ 19.95 • 144 Pages

Metal Working (Back to Shop Class)

Real World Know-How You Wish You Learned in High School

By Skills Institute Press

With this book, the handy homeowner gets to go back to school to learn how to tackle metalworking projects and repairs around the house, saving money and guaranteeing good results.

ISBN: 978-1-56523-540-3
$19.95 • 136 Pages

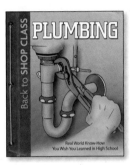

Plumbing (Back to Shop Class)

Real World Know-How You Wish You Learned in High School

By Skills Institute Press

From simple repairs to major renovations, this book helps readers save time, money, and frustration by teaching them to do the most common plumbing repairs themselves.

ISBN: 978-1-56523-588-5
$ 19.95 • 160 Pages

Outdoor Furniture (Built to Last)

14 Timeless Woodworking Projects for the Yard, Deck, and Patio

By Skills Institute Press

Design and build beautiful wooden outdoor furniture sturdy enough to withstand Mother Nature with the detailed techniques and step by step instructions in this handy guide.

ISBN: 978-1-56523-500-7
$19.95 • 144 Pages

Tumbleweed DIY Book of Backyard Sheds & Tiny Houses

Build your own guest cottage, writing studio, home office, craft workshop, or personal retreat

By Jay Shafer

Real-world plans for very handsome tiny buildings you will actually want to build, use, and enjoy.

ISBN: 978-1-56523-704-9
$19.95 • 144 Pages